Eat with Us!

A cookbook for the **Busy Woman/Mom**! Or for those who **SIMPLY** want to cook.

Many of these recipes I have had for years and used with my family. A mom and wife needs something quick, easy and delicious. I have included canning and bread in case you are feeling adventurous! I even included grandma's cookies and salve. The cookies are delicious and the salve really works. Hopefully, these recipes will make your life easier. The book is formatted for binding.

Melanie

New Orleans French Bread

Ingredients:

2 Tbsp. shortening or butter

1 Tbsp. sugar

1 Tbsp. salt

1 cup boiling water

1 cup cold water

1 pkg. dry yeast (2 ¼ tsp)

5 ½ to 6 cups flour

Directions:

Combine shortening/butter, sugar, salt and boiling water in a large bowl, stirring occasionally to melt shortening. Add cold water; cool mixture to 105 to 110 degrees. Sprinkle yeast over mixture and let stand 5 minutes, stirring to dissolve. Gradually beat in 4 cups of flour. Add enough of the remaining flour to form a stiff dough.

Turn out onto a floured surface. Knead until smooth and elastic, about 5 minutes. Place in a well-greased, turning once to grease top. Cover and let rise in a warm (85 degree) place, free from draft for 1 ½ to 2 hours or until doubled in bulk. Punch down, cover, and let rise in warm place until more than doubled in bulk.

Turn dough onto a floured surface, knead slightly to press out bubbles. Shape into a 14" to 16" cylinder on a large greased baking sheet. Cover and let rise in a warm place until doubled in bulk.

Cut ¼" deep slashes in top of dough with a sharp knife; brush with egg white glaze. Bake at 375 degrees for 40 to 50 minutes or until golden brown.

Egg White Glaze

1 egg white

2 Tbsp. water

Combine and beat until frothy.

Braided White Bread

Ingredients:

1 pkg. dry yeast

2 cups warm water (105° to 115°)

1/3 cup sugar

2 tsp salt

1 egg, well beaten

6 – 7 cups flour

3 Tbsp. oil

Directions:

Combine yeast, water, sugar, salt and egg in a large bowl; set aside for 5 minutes. Gradually add 3 cups flour, beat well. Add oil and 3 to 4 cups flour to form stiff dough.

Turn dough out on a floured surface and knead until smooth and elastic, 5 to 8 minutes. Place in

a well-greased bowl, turning to grease top. Cover and let rise in a warm (85°) place free from draft, 1 ½ to 2 hours or until doubled in bulk.
Punch dough down and divide into thirds. Shape each part into a 14" to 16" rope. Place ropes on a greased baking sheet.   Firmly pinched ends together and one end to seal.

Place right rope over center rope alternately bring each outside rope to center, as in braiding. Pinch ends to seal when braided. Cover and let rise in a warm place free from draft until doubled in bulk. Bake in 350 degree oven for 20 to 25 minutes or until lightly browned.

Sour Dough Starter

Ingredients:

1 pkg. dry yeast (2 ¼ tsp)

3 cups warm water (105° - 115°)

3 ½ cups flour

Directions:

Dissolve yeast in warm water; set aside for 5 minutes. Gradually add flour, beating on medium speed until smooth. Cover with plastic wrap. Place in a warm spot (85°), free from draft, for 24 hours or until bubbles appear on surface. (If starter has not begun to ferment after 24 hours, discard it and start over.) Will swell and then do down. Stir well, cover and return to warm place. Let stand 2 days or until foamy. Stir well. Pour into and airtight glass container and store in refrigerator. Stir before using. Yields about 4 cups.

To replenish starter after 1 cup has been removed, add 1 cup lukewarm water, ½ cup flour, and 1 tsp sugar. Cover and let stand over night or until mixture bubbles. Stir down. Store loosely covered in refrigerator. Stir before using.

Whole Wheat Sour Dough Bread

Ingredients:

1 ½ cup boiling water

½ cup shortening

1 pkg. dry yeast (2 ¼)

1 tsp sugar

1 egg, well beaten

1//2 cup salt

½ cup sugar

1 cup sourdough starter, room temperature

2 cups flour

2 cups whole wheat flour

Directions:

Combine boiling water and shortening in a large bowl. Cool to 105° to 115°. Add yeast and 1 teaspoon sugar; let stand 15 minutes. Add egg, ½ cu sugar, salt, sour dough starter and 2 ½ cups flour. Bear on medium speed for 3 minutes. Gradually stir in ½ cup flour and the whole wheat flour.

Turn dough out on a floured surface and knead about 5 minutes or until smooth and elastic.
Place dough in a greased bowl, turning to grease top. Cover and let rise in a warm (85°) place free from draft for 1 ½ to 2 hours or until doubled in bulk. Punch down.

Divide dough in half; place on a floured surface. Roll each half into an 8" x 18" rectangle. Roll up, beginning at the narrow edge. Pinch seam and ends together to seal. Place seam side down in well-greased loaf pans.

Cover and let rise in a warm place free from draft until doubled in bulk. Place in cold oven. Bake at 400 degrees for 15 minutes; reduce heat to 350 degrees and continue baking for 20 minutes or until loaves sound hollow when tapped.

Basic Sweet Dough

Ingredients:

2 pkg. yeast (4 /2 tsp)

¼ cup lukewarm water

1 cup milk

½ cup sugar

5 cups flour approx.

2 tsp salt

¼ cup shortening.

2 eggs

1 tsp grated lemon rind

Directions:

Soften yeast in lukewarm water. Scald milk. Add sugar, salt and shortening. Cool to lukewarm. Add part of the flour to make a thick batter. Mix well. Add softened yeast and eggs. Beat well. And enough flour to make a soft dough.

Turn out onto a lightly floured board and knead until smooth and satiny with tiny gas bubbles under the surface. Place in a greased bowl. Cover and let rise in a warm place until doubled, about 1 ½ hours.

Place in a greased bowl. Cover and let stand 10 minutes and shapes into tea rings, rolls or coffee cakes. Let rise until doubled in size, about 1 hour. Bake at 350 degrees for 30 minutes for coffee cake, 25 minutes for pan rolls and 20 minutes for individual rolls. Makes approximately 3 coffee cakes or 3 1//2 dozen rolls.

Cinnamon Rolls

Ingredients:

1 recipe basic sweet dough

¼ cup melted butter

1 cup sugar

1 Tbsp. cinnamon

½ cup raisins (if desired)

2 Tbsp. milk

Directions:

When basic sweet dough is light, punch down. Let stand 10 minutes. Roll into narrow sheet 1/4" thick and 6" wide. Brush with melted butter. Ix sugar and cinnamon and sprinkle over dough. Save 3 Tbsp. for top of roll. Raisins may be added if desired.

Roll up like jelly roll and seal edge. Cut into inch thick slices. Place cut side down into well-greased

12

muffin pans, ring mold or deep layer pan. Brush top with milk and sprinkle with cinnamon sugar mixture. Let rise until doubled...about 45 minutes. Bake in 350 degree oven for 25 minutes. Makes about 3 ½ dozen.

Doughnuts

Ingredients:

1 egg, beaten

1 cup of warm milk, 105 degrees

¼ cup butter, melted

¼ cup sugar

1 pkg. yeast (2 ¼ tsp)

1 tsp salt

3 cups flour

1 tsp vanilla

Directions:

Combine milk and sugar. Add yeast and stir to combine. Let rest for 5 minutes. Add egg, vanilla and butter. While beating add flour and salt. Put into greased bowl, turning to grease top. Cover and let rise until doubled in size.

Turn out onto well-floured surface and roll ½" thick. Cut into doughnuts, reserving doughnut holes. Place on floured baking sheets and let rise until doubled.

Heat oil in pot to 375 degrees. Gently place donuts in hot oil. After 1 minute flip over and cook until golden brown. Holes cook faster.

Donut Glaze

Ingredients:

4 Tbsp. butter

3 cups powdered sugar

1 tsp vanilla

½ cup milk

Directions:

Mix all ingredients together, adding enough milk to make a nice thin icing. Dip donuts in icing and cool on a rack.

Jelly Roll

Ingredients:

¾ cup flour

¾ tsp baking powder

¼ tsp salt

4 eggs (at room temperature)

¾ cup sugar

1 tsp vanilla

1 cup tart jelly

Directions:

Sift flour and measure. Combine baking powder, salt and eggs in bowl and beat. Add sugar until mixture becomes thick and light colored. Fold in flour and vanilla. Turn into 15" x 10" pan which has been lined with parchment paper. Bake at 400 degree for 13 minutes.

Turn cake out onto cloth and dust with powdered sugar. Cut off crisp edges of cake. Roll cake and cloth together and let cool 10 minutes. Unroll and spread with jelly and roll again.

Biscuits

Ingredients:

2 Cups flour

3 Tsp baking powder

1 Tsp salt

1 Tsp sugar

¼ cup shortening or butter

7/8 cup of milk (1 cup less 2 tablespoons)

Directions:

Sift together flour, baking powder, salt and sugar. Cut shortening/butter into flour mixture until fine as coarse crumbs. Add milk and stir with a fork.

Turn out onto lightly floured surface and knead until smooth. Roll dough to about ½" thick and cut with floured biscuit cutter. Bake on lightly greased baking sheet at 450 degrees for 10 – 12 minutes.

Buttermilk Biscuits

Follow recipe for biscuits, but cut baking powder to 2 teaspoons and add ¼ teaspoon of baking soda. Use 1 cup of buttermilk instead of milk.

Pancakes

Ingredients:

2 cups flour

3 tsp baking soda

¼ tsp salt

1 Tbsp. sugar

1 Tbsp. butter, melted

1 – 1 ¼ cup milk

Directions:

Mix dry ingredients, add butter and milk and mix well. Spoon onto hot griddle. When bubbles form on top, flip and cook until golden brown.

Cranberry Fruit Nut Bread

Ingredients:

2 cups flour

1 cup sugar

1 ½ tsp baking powder

½ tsp baking soda

1 tsp salt

¼ cup shortening/butter

¾ cup orange juice

1 Tbsp. grated orange rind

1 egg well beaten

½ cup of chopped nuts (walnuts are really good)

2 cups cranberries coarsely chopped

Directions:

Sift together flour, sugar, baking powder, soda and salt.   Cut in shortening until mixture resembles coarse cornmeal. Combine orange juice and grated with well beaten egg.   Pour mixture into dry ingredients, mixing just until dampened. Carefully fold in chopped nuts and cranberries. Spoon into two greased loaf pans. Spread corners and sides slightly higher than center. Bake in 350 degree oven for approximately 1 hour...until crust is golden brown and toothpick inserted in center comes out clean.

Banana Nut Bread

Ingredients:

½ cup shortening

1 ½ cups sugar

2 cups flour

½ tsp salt

½ tsp baking soda

½ tsp baking powder

2 eggs, unbeaten

4 Tbsp. milk

2 large ripe bananas, mashed

½ cup walnuts, chopped

Directions:

Cream shortening and sugar. Sift dry ingredients and add to creamed mixture. Add one egg at a time and mix well. Add milk, bananas and nuts.

Bake in a greased loaf pan at 350 degrees for 1 hour or until toothpick inserted in center comes out clean.

Jeans Gingerbread

Ingredients:

½ cup shortening

1 cup brown sugar, firmly packed

2 eggs

2 cups flour

1 tsp baking soda

1 tsp ginger

1 tsp cinnamon

¼ tsp cloves

1 tsp salt

½ cup molasses

½ cup boiling water

Directions:

Beat together shortening and sugar. Add eggs one at a time, beating well after each addition. Combine flour, soda, ginger, cinnamon, cloves and salt. Set aside.

Mix together molasses and water. Add alternately to creamed mixture. Begin and end with dry ingredients. Pour into greased and floured 13" x 9" pan at 350 degrees for 45 minutes.

Pumpkin Bread

Ingredients:

3 ½ cup flour

2 cups sugar

2 tsp baking soda

1 tsp salt

1 tsp cinnamon

½ cup nuts

2 cups pumpkin

4 eggs

1 cup oil

2 - 3 cups water

1 tsp vanilla

Directions:

Combine and sift all dry ingredients and make a well in it. Add rest of recipe in well, except nuts.

Mix until smooth, then add nuts. Pour into three well-greased loaf pans. Bake 1 hour at 250 degrees or toothpick inserted comes out clean.

Chocolate Squash Bread

Ingredients:

1 cup flour

½ cup cocoa

1 tsp baking soda

½ tsp salt

2 large egg, room temperature

¼ cup unsalted butter, melted and cooled

¼ cup oil

¾ cup packed light brown sugar

1 tsp vanilla

1 ½ cups packed shredded zucchini or yellow
squash, seeds removed

1 cup semisweet chocolate chips, divided

Directions:

Whisk together flour, cocoa powder, baking soda and salt, set aside. In large bowl, mix eggs, melted butter, oil, vanilla and brown sugar; stir until smooth. Stir dry ingredients into the wet ingredients, but do not overmix. Stir in shredded squash until just combined. Stir in ¾ cup chocolate chips.

Pour batter into greased loaf pan and sprinkle with remaining chocolate chips. Bake at 350 degrees for 50 – 60 minutes or until toothpick inserted in center comes out clean.

Persimmon Bread

Ingredients:

3 ½ cup flour

1 ½ tsp salt

2 tsp baking soda

1 tsp nutmeg

2 -2 ½ cup sugar

1 cup butter, melted, cooled to room temperature

4 large eggs, lightly beaten, room temperature

$^2/_3$ cup cognac, bourbon or whiskey

2 cups persimmon puree

2 cups walnuts or pecans, toasted and chopped

2 cups raisins or other dried fruits, diced (apricots, cranberries, dates)

Directions:

Sift together flour, salt, baking soda and nutmeg in a large bowl. Make well in center and stir in butter, eggs, liquor and persimmon puree. Add nuts and raisins. Pour into 2 buttered loaf pans and bake at 350 degrees for 1 hours or until toothpick inserted in middle comes out clean.

Jalapeno Corn Bread

Ingredients:

2 eggs

1 tsp salt

1/3 cup grated cheddar cheese

1 cup cream corn

¼ cup oil

1 cup buttermilk

2 tsp baking powder

1 cup corn meal

3 – 4 jalapeno pepper, chopped

Directions:

Mix ingredients and pour into cake pan. Cook 1 hour at 350 degrees.

Molasses Cake

Ingredients:

1 cup sugar

1 cup butter

3 eggs

1 cup molasses

2 cup flour

½ tsp ground cloves

½ tsp ginger

1 tsp cinnamon

½ tsp salt

2 tsp baking soda

1 cup boiling water

Directions:

Cream the butter and sugar. Add well beaten eggs. Add molasses. Sift the flour with cloves, ginger, cinnamon and salt. Put the soda in the cup of boiling water. Add flour mixture to the wet mixture. Gradually add the soda water, stirring constantly. Beast mixture well. The batter will be very thin, but do not add more flour.

Pour into a greased and lightly floured 9" x 13" pan. Bake in moderate oven for 45 minutes or until the cake springs bake when pressed in center.

Black Walnut Cake

Ingredients:

2 cups brown sugar

½ cup butter

2 eggs, separated and beaten

1 cup black walnuts, chopped

2/3 cup milk

2 cups flour

3 tsp baking powder

½ tsp salt

1 tsp vanilla

Directions:

Cream butter and sugar. Add egg yolks and nuts. Sift dry ingredients. Add to creamed mixture alternately with milk. Add vanilla. Fold in egg whites. Pour into loaf pan or Bundt pan and bake in 350 degree oven for 70 minutes or until toothpick inserted in center comes out clean.

Lemon Pecan Cake

Ingredients:

2 ¼ cups brown sugar

4 sticks butter

½ pound candied cherries

½ pound candied pineapple

6 eggs, beaten

4 cups flour

1 pound pecans

2 oz. lemon extract

Directions:

Mix butter and sugar well and add beaten eggs and extract. Add 2 cups flour and mix. Add 2 cups flour to fruit and nuts. Add to wet mixture. Pour into greased and floured Bundt pan and bake in 250 degree oven for 2 ½ hours or until toothpick inserted comes out clean.

Fruit Cocktail Cake

Ingredients:

1 ½ cup sugar

2 cups flour

2 tsp baking soda

¼ tsp salt

2 eggs

1 can fruit cocktail

½ cup pecans, chopped

¾ cup brown sugar

Directions:

Mix dry ingredients. Add eggs and then fruit cocktail, mix well. Pour into greased and floured 9" x 13" baking pan. Sprinkle nuts and brown sugar on top. Bake at 350 degrees for 40 minutes.

Fruit Cocktail Cake Icing

Ingredients:

1 stick butter

¾ cup sugar

½ cup milk

1 tsp vanilla

1 cup coconut

Directions:

Put butter, sugar and milk into saucepan and bring to boil. Cook 2 minutes then add vanilla and coconut. Pour over cake while hot.

Potato Cake

Ingredients:

4 eggs

2 cups sugar

1 cup butter

1 cup pecans, chopped

1 cup milk

1 cup hot mashed potatoes

2 cup flour

1 tsp vanilla

½ cup melted semi-sweet chocolate (2 ½ squares)

¼ cup nutmeg

3 tsp baking powder

Directions:

Cream together the butter and sugar. Add beaten
egg yolks, melted chocolate and mashed potatoes.

Mix flour baking powder and nutmeg. Reserve ¼ cup of flour mixture and add to nut meats. Add alternate milk and flour mixture to wet mixture. Fold in floured nuts and stiffly beaten egg whites. Pour into greased and floured cake pans. Bake at 375 degrees for 20 minutes.

Potato Cake Filling

Ingredients:

1 cup evaporated milk

1 cup sugar

1 cup coconut

1 cup nuts

4 egg yolks

1 Tbsp. butter

Directions:

Put cream, sugar, eggs and butter in saucepan and cook until thick. Add coconut and nuts. Spread between cake layers and on top.

Bourbon Pecan Cake

Ingredients:

2 cups whole candied cherries

2 cups white seedless raisins

2 cups bourbon

2 cups softened butter

2 cups sugar

2 cups packed dark brown sugar

8 eggs separated

5 cups flour

4 cups pecan halves

1 ½ tsp baking powder

2 tsp ground nutmeg

1 tsp salt

Directions:

Combine cherries, raisins and bourbon in a large mixing bowl, cover tightly and let stand in the refrigerator overnight. Drain fruits and reserve bourbon.

Place butter in a large bowl and beat on medium speed until light and fluffy. Add sugars gradually, beating on medium until well blended. Combine ½ cup of the flour with the pecans. Sift the remaining flour with the baking powder, salt and nutmeg. Add 2 cups of the flour mixture to butter and mix thoroughly. Add the reserve bourbon and the remainder of the flour mixture alternately, ending with the flour. Beat well after each addition.

Beat egg whites until stiff and fold gently into cake batter. Add drained fruits and floured nuts to cake batter, blend thoroughly. Grease a 10 tube cake or Bundt pan. Line bottom with wax paper.

Pour cake batter into pan to within one inch of the top. (The remaining batter may be baked in a small loaf pan.) Bake in a 275 degree oven for 4 hours or until toothpick inserted in center comes out clean. Bake loaf cake 1 ½ hours.

Feathery Crumb Cake

Ingredients:

1 cup butter

1 cup sugar

1 cup packed brown sugar

3 cups flour

Directions:

Add:

1 tsp baking powder

1 tsp baking soda

1 tsp cinnamon

½ tsp cloves

½ tsp allspice

½ tsp nutmeg

¼ tsp salt

Directions:

Mix first four ingredients until coarse crumbs. Remove and reserve one cup for crumb topping.

Stir in 1 cup of soured milk, buttermilk or milk until smooth. Pour into greased and lightly floured 13" x 9" baking pan. Smooth batter and sprinkle with reserved crumb topping. Bake at 350 degrees for 45 minutes.

Chocolate Sheet Cake

Ingredients:

2 cups sugar

2 cups flour

$1/3$ cup cocoa

1 tsp baking soda

½ tsp salt

1 cup butter

1 cup water

½ buttermilk

2 eggs

1 tsp vanilla

Directions:

Combine sugar, flour, cocoa, baking soda, and salt in a large mixing bowl. Mix well. Heat margarine and water in a saucepan until boiling. Pour over dry ingredients and mix. Beat in buttermilk, eggs and vanilla. Pour thin batter in greased and floured 15" x 10" pan. Bake in 400 degree oven for 20 minutes.

Sheet Cake Frosting

Ingredients:

½ cup butter

¼ cup cocoa

6 Tbsp. milk

4 cups powdered sugar

1 cup walnuts

Directions:

Combine butter, cocoa and milk in saucepan. Heat to boiling. Pour over sugar and nuts. Mix well. Spread on hot cake.

Fresh Apple Cake

Ingredients:

3 cups flour

1 ½ tsp baking soda

1 tsp salt

2 cups sugar

1 ½ cups butter

3 cups fresh apples, chopped

1 cup pecans, chopped

2 tsp vanilla

2 eggs, beaten

Directions:

Mix flour, baking soda, salt and sugar together. Cream in butter. Add vanilla and eggs. Stir in nuts. Pour into Bundt pan and bake in 325 degree oven for 1 hour.

Fresh Apple Cake Icing

Ingredients:

1 cup powdered sugar

1 egg

½ cup butter

Directions:

Put ingredients in saucepan and heat until butter melted, stirring constantly. Pour over cake.

Dump Cake

Ingredients:

1 can cherry pie filling

1 can crushed pineapple

1 white cake mix

½ cup butter

1 cup pecans, chopped small

Directions:

Butter bottom of pan. Put ingredients in square cake pan in order. Bake at 325 degrees for 45 minutes.

Rum Cake

Ingredients:

1 cup pecans, chopped

1 yellow cake mix

1 – 3 ¾ oz. vanilla instant pudding mix

4 eggs

½ cup water

½ cup oil

½ cup dark rum

Directions:

Butter Bundt pan. Spread pecans around the bottom of pan. Mix rest of ingredients together and add to pan. Bake at 325 degrees for 1 hour or until toothpick inserted comes out clean.

Rum Cake Topping

Ingredients:

½ cup butter

½ cup rum

¼ cup water

1 cup sugar

Directions:

Combine ingredients in saucepan and bring to boil over medium heat. Cook for 5 minutes, stirring constantly. Remove from heat and pour over cake.

Kentucky Prune Cake

Ingredients:

1 ½ cups sugar

1 cup oil

2 cups flour

1 tsp cinnamon

½ tsp nutmeg

½ tsp salt

½ tsp allspice

1 tsp soda

1 cup buttermilk

12 tsp vanilla

1 cup prunes, cooked and chopped

1 cup nut, chopped

Directions:

Combine ingredients in order listed. Put in greased and floured 9" x 13" baking pan. Bake at 300 degree until sides shrink and top springs back, approximately 45 minutes to 1 hour.

Date Bar Cake

Ingredients:

1 cup dates, chopped

1 cup walnuts, chopped

2 cups flour

½ cups butter

1 ½ cups sugar

½ tsp baking soda

1 cup warm water

2 eggs, beaten

1 Tbsp. cocoa

1 tsp vanilla

Directions:

Sift flour, sugar and cocoa together. Mix baking soda and water. Mix together butter, eggs, water mixture and vanilla. Stir flour mixture into wet ingredients. Pour into loaf pans. Bake in 350 degree oven for 45 minutes to 1 hour.

Date Bar Cake Icing

Ingredients:

1 cup dates, chopped

1 cup nuts, chopped

1 ¾ cup sugar

3 cups milk

Directions:

Combine ingredients in saucepan. Boil until mixture scrapes up easily from bottom of pan. Pour over cake.

White Birthday Cake

Ingredients:

2 ½ cup flour

3 ¼ tsp baking powder

1 tsp salt

1 ¼ cup sugar

½ cup butter

2/3 cup milk

1/3 cup milk

½ cup egg whites, unbeaten (4 – 6 eggs)

1 tsp vanilla

Directions:

Combine flour, baking powder, salt and sugar and sift into bowl. Add shortening and 2/3 cup of milk, beat for 2 minutes on low speed. Add 1/3 cup of milk, egg whites and vanilla and beat again for 3 to 4 minutes on medium speed. Pour into

lightly greased 8" cake pans. Bake at 350 degrees
for 35 minutes.

Seven Minute Frosting

Ingredients:

2 egg whites

1 ½ cup sugar

1 ½ tsp corn syrup or ¼ tsp cream of tartar

$1/3$ cup cold water

$1/8$ tsp salt

1 tsp vanilla

Directions:

Combine egg whites, sugar, corn syrup or cream of tartar, water and salt in top of double boiler. Beat for 1 minute to mix and then beat constantly for 7 minutes on high. Beat in vanilla.

Chocolate Meringue Pie

Pie Crust

Ingredients:

1 cup flour

½ tsp salt

1/3 cup shortening or butter, cold

3 - 4 Tbsp. ice water

Directions:

Combine flour and salt. Cut shortening in with a pastry blender or fork until mixture resembles coarse crumbs. Drizzle water into bowl 1 Tbsp. at a time until dough forms a ball.

Turn out onto lightly floured surface and roll $1/8$" thick. Place in 9" pie plate; trim edges and crimp. Prick bottom and sides with a fork and bake at 450 degrees for 9 minutes.

Chocolate Filling

Ingredients:

1 cup sugar

¼ cup plus 1 tsp cornstarch

¼ cup unsweetened cocoa

¼ tsp salt

1 ½ cup milk

½ cup evaporated milk

4 large egg yolks, beaten

2 Tbsp. butter

1 Tbsp. vanilla

Directions:

In a medium saucepan combine sugar, cornstarch, cocoa and salt. Gradually whisk in milks. Whisking constantly, cook over medium-high heat until mixture comes to a boil; continue boiling and whisking for 1 minute. Remove from heat and gradually whisk into the egg yolks. Cook over medium heat, whisking constantly, for 3 minutes.

Meringue

Ingredients:

5 large egg whites, room temperature

¼ tsp cream of tartar

¼ cup sugar

Directions:

Beat egg whites and cream of tartar until foamy.

Easy Chocolate Pie

Ingredients:

12 oz. semi-sweet chocolate chips

$1/_3$ cup water

8 oz. cream cheese, softened

1 – 12 oz. tub whipped topping

¼ cup sugar

1 graham cracker crust

Directions:

Melt chocolate chips with water in double boiler. Let cool. Beat cream cheese and sugar until smooth. Add melted chocolate. Fold in 3 ½ cups whipped topping. Spoon into crust. Top with remaining whipped topping. Chill about 3 hours.

Pecan Pie

Ingredients:

1 pie crust, unbaked

1 cup sugar

3 Tbsp. brown sugar

½ tsp salt

1 cup corn syrup

¾ tsp vanilla

$1/_3$ cup butter, melted

3 eggs, beaten

1 ¼ cup pecans, chopped

Directions:

Combine all ingredients, except pecans. Mix well.
Pour pecan in bottom of unbaked pie crust. Pour
syrup mixture over the top. Cover lightly with foil
and bake at 350 degrees for 30 minutes. Remove
foil and bake for 20 minutes or until set.

Pumpkin Pie

Ingredients:

1 – 15 oz. can pumpkin

1 ¼ cup heavy cream

2/3 cup sugar

3 large eggs

1 tsp cinnamon

1 ½ tsp ground nutmeg

½ tsp vanilla

¼ tsp salt

2 Tbsp. butter, softened

Directions:

Line pie crust with foil and bake in 350 degree oven for 20 minutes (add dry beans to center to keep from puffing up). Remove foil and weights and continue baking until golden, approximately 10 minutes.

Gently whisk pumpkin, heavy cream, sugar, 2 eggs, cinnamon, nutmeg, vanilla, salt and butter. Pour into pie crust. Beat the remaining egg and brush pie crust with it. Bake for 50 minutes to 1 hour or until knife inserted in middle comes out clean.

Pudding Pie

Ingredients:

Large graham cracker crust

1 – 9 oz. whipped topping, frozen

1 can sweetened condensed milk

$^1/_3$ cup lemon juice

Directions:

Mix the milk and whipped topping (Do not allow to thaw!) in a large bowl with a wire whip or fork. Do not mix too much, just until smooth. Add the juice and stir until well mixed. Pour into crust and chill about 30 minutes. Top with 1 can of prepared pie filling. Keep refrigerated.

Apple Pie

Ingredients:

¼ cup brown sugar

½ cup sugar

2 Tbsp. flour

¼ tsp salt

¼ tsp cinnamon

¼ tsp nutmeg

2 Tbsp. butter

Double pie crust

Directions:

Cut apples into slices. Combine brown sugar, sugar, flour, salt, cinnamon and nutmeg. Mix apples and dry ingredients. Put in pie shell and put slices of butter over the top. Add top crust and brush shell with milk. Bake at 425 degrees for 40 to 45 minutes.

Pumpkin Pie

Ingredients:

1 ¾ cup canned or fresh pumpkin

½ tsp cinnamon

¼ tsp ginger

½ tsp nutmeg

½ tsp salt

¾ cup sugar

2 eggs

2 Tbsp. butter, melted

1 ½ cup evaporated milk, 2 cans

1 pie crust

Directions:

Mix all ingredients and pour into pie crust. Bake at 425 degrees for 15 minutes. Lower temperature to 350 degrees and bake for 40 to 50

minutes or until knife inserted in middle comes
out clean.

Mock Apple Pie

Ingredients:

1 ½ cup water

1 ½ cup sugar

1 ½ tsp cinnamon

1 ½ tsp cream of tartar

Ritz crackers

Double pie crust

Directions:

Combine water, sugar, cinnamon and cream of tartar in saucepan and boil for 1 minute. Crumble 16 crackers into bottom crust. Pour mixture over the top. Add top crust. Bake at 425 degrees until golden brown.

Peaches and Cream Pie

Ingredients:

7 or 8 peach halves

2/3 cup sugar

4 Tbsp. flour

¼ tsp salt

½ tsp cinnamon

1 can evaporated milk

Pie crust

Directions:

Place peaches round side up in bottom of pie crust. Combine dry ingredients, add evaporated milk and mix well. Pour into pie shell. Bake at 400 degrees for 35 to 45 or minutes or until set.

Vinegar Pie

Ingredients:

¼ cup vinegar

2 cups water

1 cup sugar

1 tsp lemon juice

1 tsp butter

5 Tbsp. flour

2 egg yolks

Pie crust

Directions:

Boil vinegar and water together for 1 minute, cool. Combine sugar, salt and flour, add egg yolks. Pour into vinegar water and cook until thick. Add lemon juice and butter and pour into pie shell. Top with meringue.

Meringue Topping

Ingredients:

2 egg whites, beaten

4 Tbsp. sugar

1/8 tsp cream of tartar

Directions:

Beat egg whites until stiff peaks form. Mix in cream of tartar and sugar. Spread on top of pie.

Mystery Pie

Ingredients:

20 Hi Ho cracker

1 cup sugar

1 cup milk

3 egg whites, beat stiff

1 tsp baking powder

Pie crust

Directions:

Mix sugar, milk, and baking powder. Mix in cracker. Stir in egg whites. Pour into pie crust and bake at 300 degrees for 30 minutes. Top with whipped topping.

Fried Pies

Ingredients:

2 ½ cups flour

1 tsp salt

1 tsp sugar

½ tsp baking powder

½ cup shortening or butter

¾ cup evaporated milk

1 egg, beaten

Directions:

Combine dry ingredients. Cut in shortening. Mix in milk and egg. Turn out onto floured surface and roll 1/8" thick. Cut 4" x 6" pieces and fill with fruit filling. Drop in hot oil until golden brown. Yields 18

Pie Crust

Ingredients:

3 cups flour

1 ¼ cup shortening

1 tsp salt

1 tsp vinegar

1 egg, beaten

½ cup cold water

Directions:

Mix all ingredients together. Make 4 large crust.

Pie Crust for Freezer

Ingredients;

5 lbs. flour

3 lbs. shortening

3 cups water

1 cup corn syrup

2 tsp salt

Directions:

Mix ingredients together. Form into balls sized for pie crust. Put on cookie sheet and freeze, then bag to freeze.

Grandma's Cookies

Ingredients:

¾ cup shortening, softened

1 cup brown sugar

½ cup sugar

1 egg

¼ cup water

1 cup flour, sifted

1 tsp vanilla

1 tsp salt

½ tsp soda

3 cups oatmeal

Directions:

Combine shortening, brown sugar, sugar, egg, water and vanilla; beat thoroughly. Sift together flour, salt and soda. Add to shortening mixture and mix well. Stir in dry oats and mix well.

Drop by teaspoon full onto shiny cookie sheet or one covered with foil. Bake at 350 degrees for 12 to15 minutes. They should puff up in middle. Yields 3 to 4 dozen.

Pumpkin Cookies

Ingredients:

$^{1}/_{3}$ cup oil

3 eggs, beaten

1 tsp vanilla

1 $^{1}/_{3}$ cup sugar

1 can pumpkin

2 ½ cup flour

1 tsp salt

¼ tsp allspice

1 tsp cinnamon

½ cup nuts, chopped

4 tsp baking powder

¼ tsp ginger

1 cup raisins

Directions:

Mix together oil, eggs, vanilla, sugar and pumpkin, mix well. In separate bowl mix flour, salt, allspice, cinnamon, nuts, baking powder, ginger and raisins. Combine all ingredients and drop by spoonful onto greased baking sheet. Bake at 400 degrees for 12 minutes.

Molasses Cookies

Ingredients:

½ cup shortening or butter

½ cup sugar

1 egg, beaten

1 cup molasses

3 cups flour

½ tsp baking soda

3 tsp baking powder

1 tsp salt

4 Tbsp. buttermilk

Directions:

Cream shortening and sugar, add beaten egg and molasses and mix well. Mix dry ingredients, then add alternately with buttermilk. Mix into a dough.

Drop by spoonful's onto a greased cookie sheet. Bake at 400 degrees for 10 minutes. Make 7 dozen.

Snickerdoodles

Ingredients:

1 cup shortening or butter

1 ½ cups sugar

2 eggs

2 ¾ cups flour

2 tsp cream of tartar

1 tsp baking soda

¼ tsp sugar

2 tsp cinnamon

Directions:

Mix shortening, sugar and eggs together. Separately mix flour, cream of tartar, baking soda and salt. Stir into shortening mixture. Shape into 1" balls. Mix together ¼ tsp sugar and cinnamon. Roll balls in mixture and place 2" apart on ungreased baking sheet. Bake at 400 degrees for 8 to 10 minutes.

Sugar Cookie

Ingredients:

1 cup sugar

¾ cup shortening or butter

2 eggs

1 tsp salt

1 tsp vanilla or lemon extract

2 ½ cups flour

1 tsp baking powder

Directions:

Mix shortening, sugar, eggs and flavoring. Blend in flour, baking powder, and salt. Cover and chill for one hour. Turn out on lightly floured surface and roll dough to $1/8$" to ¼" thick. Cut and place on cookie sheet. Bake at 375 degrees for 7 to 9 minutes.

Chocolate Chip Brownies

Ingredients:

12 oz. pkg. semi-sweet chocolate chips, divided

1 stick butter, sliced

3 large eggs

1 ¼ cup flour

1 cup sugar

1 tsp vanilla

¼ tsp baking soda

½ cup nuts, chopped

Directions:

Melt 1 cup chocolate chips and butter in saucepan over low heat until smooth. Stir in eggs. Stir in flour, sugar, vanilla and baking soda. Then stir in remaining 1 cup chocolate chips and nuts. (For a more cakelike brownie, add all chocolate chips with butter.) Spread into 9" x 13" baking dish and bake at 350 degrees for 20 to 25 minutes, until toothpick inserted comes out only slightly sticky...clean if all chips added at once.

Squash Brownies

Ingredients:

1 ½ cup sugar

½ cup oil

2 cups flour

¼ cup unsweetened cocoa

2 cups shredded squash, seeded (don't squeeze)

2 tsp vanilla

1 tsp salt

1 ½ tsp baking soda

1 ¼ cup semi-sweet chocolate chips, divided

Directions:

Combine sugar, oil and flour until mixture resembles wet sand. While mixing on low, add cocoa, zucchini, vanilla, salt and baking soda; mix well. Stir in 1 cup chocolate chips.

Pour mixture into greased 9" x 13" baking pan. Bake at 350 degrees for 25 to 30 minutes or until toothpick inserted in center comes out clean.

Vanilla Ice Cream

Ingredients:

1 tsp vanilla

6 eggs, beaten

4 cans evaporated milk

2 ½ cup sugar

Directions:

Place in ice cream freezer and churn until thick. May add fruit and flavored sodas.

Cajeta (Ca-he-ta)
(Caramel Sauce)

Ingredients:

2 qts. goat's milk or whole cow's milk

2 cups sugar

2" piece of cinnamon stick, preferably Mexican canela

½ tsp baking soda

1 Tbsp. water

Directions:

In medium saucepan, combine milk, sugar and cinnamon stick. Cook over medium heat stirring regularly until milk comes to a simmer and sugar dissolved. Remove from heat.

Dissolve baking soda in water. Stir into milk mixture. Return to heat and maintain brisk simmer, stirring regularly until mixture turns pale golden...approximately 1 hour. Continue cooking and stirring frequently as the mixture turn a caramel brown color and thickens to a syrup consistency.

Place a drop on plate; it should be like caramel candy. If too thick add a tablespoon or so of water. Pour through strainer into a storage container. Should keep for 1 to 2 months. Delicious over ice cream.

Banana Pudding

Ingredients:

4 large eggs

¾ cup sugar

3 Tbsp. flour

½ tsp salt

2 cups whole milk

½ tsp vanilla

30 – 40 vanilla wafers

3 – 4 ripe bananas, thinly sliced

Directions:

Separate 3 eggs and set whites aside. Add remaining egg to the yolks.

In a saucepan, whisk together ½ cup sugar, flour and salt. Stir in the yolk mixture. Stir in the milk. Cook   uncovered,   stirring   often,   until thickened...approximately 10 minutes. Remove from heat and add vanilla.

Spread thin layer of pudding in 9" x 5" (1 ½ qt.) baking dish. Place a layer of vanilla water on top. Arrange a layer of bananas over vanilla wafers. Spread $1/3$ of remaining pudding over, then layer wafers, bananas and pudding; ending with pudding.

Beat reserved egg whites with a pinch of salt until they are stiff. Gradually beat in ¼ cup sugar and continue beating until stiff peaks form. Spread the meringue over the pudding and bake in 425 degree oven for 5 minutes or until meringue is lightly browned.

Peanut Brittle

Ingredients:

2 cups sugar

1 cup corn syrup

½ cup water

2 ½ cup peanuts

1 tsp salt

1 Tbsp. butter

1 tsp vanilla

2 tsp baking soda

Directions:

Stir sugar, syrup and water in heavy skillet until sugar dissolves. Cook over medium heat to soft ball stage (234°) or until it spins a thread. Add nuts. Cook to hard crack stage (305°) until golden brown, stirring often. Add butter, vanilla, salt and baking soda. Remove from heat and add butter and soda. Pour at once into 2 buttered pans. Spread to desired thickness with spatula. Break into pieces.

Caramel Corn

Ingredients:

1 cup brown sugar

1 cup sugar

1 cup butter

½ cup corn syrup

1 tsp salt

½ tsp baking soda

1 Tbsp. butter flavor

1 Tbsp. burnt sugar flavor

Directions:

Combine brown sugar, sugar, butter, corn syrup and salt in saucepan. Boil for 5 minute. Stir in flavorings and soda. Pour over 8 quarts of popped corn. Place in a 200 degree oven, stirring often, until dry.

Divinity

Ingredients:

3 cups sugar

½ cups light corn syrup

½ cup cold water

2 egg whites

1 tsp vanilla

1 cup pecans, chopped

Directions:

Place sugar, syrup and water in heavy pan over low heat. Stir until sugar dissolves. Cook to soft ball stage. Beat egg whites until stiff. Pour half of syrup with egg whites and continue beating with egg whites and continue beating.

Put remaining syrup on stove and cook until hard ball stage. Add this mixture to egg and syrup mixture. Continue beating. Add vanilla and nuts at high speed. Beat until it begins to thicken. Drop quickly by spoonful's onto wax paper.

Strawberry Orange Punch

Ingredients:

2 bottle orange soda

2 bottles strawberry soda

1 can Hawaiian punch

Directions:

Cool and add ice.

Tropical Punch

Ingredients:

1 can red Hawaiian punch

1 – 6 oz. can frozen lemonade concentrate

1 – 6 oz. can frozen orange juice concentrate

1 - 6 oz. can frozen grape juice concentrate

6 cups cold water

1 bottle ginger ale, 3 ½ cups

Directions:

Combine juices, punch and water and pour over ice. With bottle resting on side carefully pour in ginger ale. 30 to 35 servings.

Pineapple Punch

Ingredients:

6 cans Sprite

½ gallon pineapple sherbet

Directions:

Fold ingredients together.

Dill Pickles

Ingredients:

5 pints water

1 pint vinegar

½ cup salt

Directions:

Combine and heat to boiling. Fill quart jar with cucumber and pour water mixture over. Add a grape leaf, a head of dill and a clove of garlic to the jar. Put lid on and process in hot water bath for 15 minutes.

Picante Sauce

Ingredients:

9 – 10 large ripe tomatoes

1 large onion, quartered

1 small carrot, sliced

½ cup jalapeno peppers, chopped

½ cup chile peppers, finely chopped

½ tsp pepper

1 ½ tsp pickling salt

1 Tbsp. garlic salt

Directions:

Place tomatoes, onion and carrots in blend and process until finely chopped. Add remaining ingredients. Pour into saucepan and simmer for 30 minutes. Pour into pint jars and put in hot water bath for 35 minutes.

Squash Relish

Ingredients:

10 cups zucchini or yellow squash, peeled and chopped with seed removed

6 – 8 onions

4 bell peppers

½ tsp green food coloring

Combine all ingredients and let stand for 30 minutes, then drain mixture.

4 cups sugar

2 cups vinegar

2 tsp celery seeds

2 tsp mustard seeds

2 tsp turmeric

½ tsp black pepper

Directions:

Mix all ingredients in large pot and boil together for 5 minutes. Pack in pint jars. Process in boiling water for 5 minutes.

Lime Sweet Pickles

Ingredients:

7 lbs. cucumbers

2 gal. water

2 cups lime

2 qt. vinegar

4 lbs. sugar

1 tsp pickling spices

1 tsp whole cloves

1 tsp celery seed

1 tsp salt

Directions:

Mix water and lime. Cut cucumbers into chunks and add to water lime mixture and let soak. Pour off lime water and rinse thoroughly. Mix remaining ingredients and add cucumbers. Simmer for 35 minutes. After cooking pack into

sterilized jars.   Reheat syrup and pour into jars.
Process in hot water bath for 15 minutes.

Crosscut Pickles

Ingredients:

4 quarts cucumbers, sliced

½ cups white onions, sliced

2 quarts crushed ice

$^1/_3$ cup salt

4 ½ cups sugar

1 ½ turmeric

2 Tbsp. mustard seed

1 ½ tsp celery seed

3 cups vinegar

Directions:

Wash and drain cucumber slices. Add onions and salt and mix thoroughly. Cover with ice and let sit 3 hours. Drain. Combine sugar and spices, add vinegar. Heat to boil, add cucumbers and onions.

Heat for 5 minutes. Put in jars and process in hot water bath for 5 minutes.

Pickled Beets

Ingredients:

Beets

2 cups water

2 cups vinegar

1 tsp cloves

1 tsp allspice

1 lemon, thinly sliced

1 Tbsp. cinnamon

Directions:

Combine all ingredients in large pot. Peel beets and cut into chunks or leave whole. Add to pot. Simmer for 15 minutes. Remove lemon slices and put into jars. Process in boiling water bath for 35 minutes.

Cajun Cabbage

Ingredients:

1 head of cabbage

1 lb. ground chuck

1 lb. boudin sausage

2 cans ranch beans

2 Rotel tomatoes

Directions:

Shred cabbage. Remove boudin from casing. Cook meat in large pot. Add cabbage, beans and Rotel. Cook stirring often until cabbage is wilted and dish is heated through.

Quick & Tasty Lasagna

Ingredients:

1 lb. ground beef

½ onion, chopped

1/2 tsp garlic salt

Large can diced or crushed tomatoes

1 small can tomato paste

1 tsp basil

1 tsp oregano

Mozzarella cheese

American cheese

Lasagna noodles

Directions:

Cook ground meat with onion. Add garlic salt, tomatoes, tomato paste, basil and oregano and simmer for 15 minutes. Cook lasagna noodles until al dente. Layer ½ sauce in bottom of 9" x 13" dish, then noodles, mozzarella cheese, noodles, American cheese and ½ sauce. Bake at 350 degrees until cheese bubbles up.

Chicken Enchiladas

Ingredients:

2 chicken breast

1 can chopped green chiles

1 can cream of chicken soup

Monterrey jack cheese

Cheddar cheese

1/3 cup milk

½ onion, chopped

Corn tortillas

Directions:

Stew chicken and chop. Soften corn tortillas in 1 Tbsp. oil in a hot skillet. Add chicken, onion, cheddar cheese and Monterrey jack cheese to each tortilla and roll up. Place in 9" x 13" dish. Mix milk and cream of chicken soup. Pour over enchiladas. Bake in 350 degree oven until sauce bubbles.

Chicken Marsala

Ingredients:

2 boneless chicken breast

3 Tbsp. flour seasoned with pepper

4 Tbsp. butter

½ lb. fresh mushrooms, sliced

2 beef bouillon

½ cup Marsala wine

Fresh parsley for garnish

Directions:

Put the meat between two pieces of wax paper and pound thin. Cut meat into serving size pieces and coat each piece with flour.

Heat butter in skillet until sizzles and add the chicken. Cook over high heat until browned on both sides and cooked through. Add sliced mushrooms and sauté briefly. Add beef bouillon and Marsala, stir everything and cook for 1 minute. Arrange on platter and pour pan juices over. Garnish with parsley.

Cajun Cabbage

Ingredients:

Head of cabbage

1 lb. ground chuck

1 lb. boudin sausage

2 cans ranch beans

2 cans Rotel tomatoes

Directions:

Remove boudin from its casing and cook with ground chuck. Thinly slice cabbage and cook until limp. Combine all ingredients in large pot and heat through.

Green Pepper Steak

Ingredients:

1 lb. beef chuck or round, fat trimmed

¼ cup soy sauce

1 clove garlic, chopped

1 ½ tsp grated fresh ginger or ½ tsp ground ginger

¼ cup oil

1 cup green onion, thinly sliced

1 cup green or red bell pepper cut into 1" squares

2 stalks celery, thinly sliced

1 Tbsp. cornstarch

1 cup water

2 tomatoes, cut into wedges

Directions:

Thinly slice beef $1/8$" thick. Combine soy sauce, garlic, ginger. Add beef and toss; set aside. Heat oil in large frying pan or wok. Add beef and toss over high heat until browned. If meat isn't tender, cover and simmer for 30 to 40 minutes over low heat. Turn up heat and add vegetables. Toss until vegetables are tender crisp, about 10 minutes. Mix cornstarch with water. Add to pan, stir and cook until thickened. Add tomatoes and heat through.

Pasta Marinara

Ingredients:

8 cloves garlic, chopped

2 Tbsp. olive oil

8 Tbsp. Romano cheese

2 large cans tomatoes, diced or crushed

16 oz. tomato sauce

14 fresh basil leaves, but chiffonade (roll and slice)

Salt and pepper, to taste

1 tsp sugar

Spiral pasta

Directions:

Cook pasta to al dente. Combine all other ingredients in pan and simmer for 30 minutes. Pour over pasta and serve

Optional: Add ¼ cup red wine and/or mushrooms

Crab Fritters

Ingredients:

1 egg, beaten

½ cup flour

½ cup milk

1 cup clams, minced

¼ tsp salt

1/8 tsp pepper

2 Tbsp. onion, minced

2 Tbsp. bell pepper, minced

½ cup oil

Directions:

Combine all ingredients. Form into 2" balls and fry.

Dinner in a Skillet

Ingredients:

1 lb. ground beef

2 eggs, slightly beaten

½ cup milk

½ cup bread crumbs or crackers

3 Tbsp. onion, chopped

1 tsp salt

½ tsp ground mustard

¼ tsp black pepper

1 can cream of tomato soup

Soup can of milk

1 can mixed vegetables

Flour

¼ cup oil

Directions:

Combine first 8 ingredients and shape into small balls and roll in flour. Heat oil in skillet and fry meatballs for about 10 minutes over medium heat. Drain oil. Mix soup and milk, add vegetables. Add to skillet and simmer for 10 minutes.

Chicken Tortilla Soup

Ingredients:

4 boneless chicken breast, cooked and chopped

2 can chicken broth

2 can Rotel

1 cup salsas

1 tsp cumin

½ cup cilantro, chopped

1 can corn

Cheddar cheese, shredded

Sour cream

Tortilla chips

Directions:

Combine all ingredients and heat through. Put in bowl, top with cheese, sour cream and tortilla chips.

King Ranch Chicken Casserole

Ingredients:

1 cup onion, chopped

¼ cup butter

1 can cream of mushroom soup

1 can cream of chicken soup

2 cups chicken, cooked and chopped

1 can Rotel

1 clove garlic, minced

1 Tbsp. chili powder

1 cup chicken broth

1 pkg. soft tortillas

1 lb. cheddar cheese, grated

Directions:

Sauté onions in butter, add soups, tomatoes, garlic and chili powder. Mix well and set aside. Cut tortillas into fourth and dip in chicken broth. Line a 9" x 13" casserole with the tortillas. Alternate layers of chopped chicken, sauce and cheese, ending with cheese. Bake at 350 degrees for 30 minutes.

Bean Burritos

Ingredients:

16 oz. refried beans

1 ½ cups salsa

1 can chopped green chiles

Flour tortillas

Cheddar cheese, grated

Lettuce, shredded

Directions:

Combine refried beans, ½ cup salsa and green chiles in medium saucepan and cook over medium heat until heated through, stirring constantly. Heat tortillas. Spoon ¼ cup bean mixture into tortilla and top with cheese, lettuce and salsa. Fold to cover filling.

Chili Rellenos

Ingredients:

6 Anaheim/Hatch chiles

8 oz. queso fresco cheese or Monterrey jack, cut into strips

2 eggs

1 tsp baking powder

1 Tbsp. milk

Oil

Directions:

Place chiles on a cookie sheet under broiler until skins blacken and peel away. Peel and remove seeds from peppers. Beat egg whites until stiff, stir in baking powder. Combine egg yolks and milk. Very gently stir egg whites into milk mixture. Stuff peppers with cheese.

Heat oil in skillet, enough to cover rellenos. Roll peppers in flour and then dip in egg/milk mixture. Fry until golden brown.

Steak Flutes

Ingredients:

Round Steak, fry and dice

4 Potatoes, diced and fried

3 Tomatoes, quartered or large dice

Flour tortillas

Directions:

Combine steak and potatoes in pan, stir in tomatoes. Sauté for 2 minutes. Roll up in flour tortilla and fry until golden brown.

Pork Chops and Orange Juice

Ingredients:

6 pork chops, fat trimmed

1 Tbsp. olive oil

1 can frozen orange juice

$2/_3$ cup water

2 Tbsp. Brown sugar

1 ½ tsp ground ginger

1 tsp Poultry seasoning

1 Tbsp. lemon juice

1 tsp salt

Directions:

Add olive oil to pan and heat. Fry pork chops until browned.   Combine orange juice, water, lemon juice and set aside. Combine brown sugar, ginger poultry seasoning and salt.

Place pork chops in 9" x 13" baking dish, pour orange juice mixture over. Sprinkle with brown sugar mixture. Cover and bake in 350 degree oven for 1 ½ hours.

Pork Chops in the Corn

Ingredients:

4 pork chops, fat trimmed

½ cup evaporated milk

¼ cup bread crumbs

1 can creamed corn

2 eggs, beaten

4 Tbsp. onion, chopped

¾ tsp salt

¼ tsp celery salt

1 Tbsp. olive oil

Directions:

Place oil in pan and heat. Season chops and brown on both sides, drain fat off. Place chops in 9" x 13" baking dish. In pan chops were cooked in, put corn, bread crumbs, milk, eggs, salt, celery salt

and onion and mix. Pour over pork chops. Bake in
325 degree oven for 45 minutes.

Stuffed Bell Peppers

Ingredients:

8 bell peppers, seeded

2 lbs. ground beef

1 small onion, chopped

2 tsp lemon juice

8 tsp tomato juice

Pinch each of thyme, salt, pepper and garlic salt

1 ½ tsp Worcestershire sauce

1 cup minute rice

1 ¼ cup cheddar cheese, grated

Directions:

Brown ground beef. Add onion, lemon juice, tomato juice, seasonings, Worcestershire and rice and cook for 15 minutes, then stir in cheese. Stuff peppers and place on baking sheet, salt tops. Bake at 350 for 25 minutes.

Potato Stew

Ingredients:

6 – 7 cups potatoes

3 cups chicken broth

1 Tbsp. butter

1 Tbsp. garlic, minced

1 onion, thinly sliced

1 cup carrots, thinly sliced

1 cup celery, finely diced

3 Tbsp. flour

2 sprigs Thyme or 1 Tbsp. dried

1 Bay leaf

3 Tbsp. parsley, finely chopped

1/8 tsp fresh ground pepper

Pinch nutmeg

1 cup milk

Salt and pepper to taste

Directions:

Combine butter, garlic, onions, carrots, and celery in large pot over medium-low heat and cook for 5 minutes. Increase heat to medium, add 2 Tbsp. flour and stir until flour is well combined. Gradually add broth and stir. Stir in thyme, bay leaf parsley, pepper and nutmeg. Add potatoes and bring to simmer. Partially cover and simmer for 15 minutes, stirring occasionally.

Whisk together remaining flour and milk, stir into soup. Simmer, stirring occasionally for 8 to 10 minutes, until soup begins to thicken. Remove from heat, season with salt and pepper, remove bay leaf and thyme sprigs.

Spaghetti

Ingredients:

1 – 20 pkg. spaghetti

2 lbs. ground beef

1 large onion, chopped

1 bell pepper, chopped

1 6 oz. can sliced mushrooms

1 can tomato sauce

1 – 6 oz. can tomato paste

1 large can crushed tomatoes

1 tsp salt

½ tsp ground mustard

½ tsp oregano

½ tsp black pepper

¼ tsp garlic powder

¼ tsp Tabasco sauce

½ tsp chili powder

1/4 tsp Worcestershire sauce

Directions:

Cook spaghetti until al dente. Brown ground beef and drain. Stir in remaining ingredients and simmer for 30 minutes. Combine with spaghetti. May be baked in 350 degree oven for 30 more minutes for more depth of flavor.

Chicken Fried Steak

Ingredients:

2 lbs. round steak, fat trimmed

3 Tbsp. sugar

½ tsp Cajun seasoning

1 egg

1 Tbsp. baking powder

2 cups milk

Oil

Flour

Directions:

Tenderize meat with mallet. Cut into 5" to 6" wide pieces. Combine sugar, Cajun seasoning, egg, baking powder and milk and mix well. Roll meat in flour, then dip in batter. Roll in flour again. Heat oil and fry for approximately 8 minutes.

Chicken Fried Steak Gravy

Ingredients:

3 Tbsp. oil

3 Tbsp. flour

2 cup water or milk

Salt and pepper to taste

Directions:

Heat skillet that steak was fried in over medium heat. Sift flour into skillet. Stir until flour is browned. Add water/milk gradually, stirring constantly until desired thickness. Add salt and pepper to taste. Serve over chicken fried steak.

Chicken Spaghetti

Ingredients:

1 package spaghetti

1 chicken, skinned and chopped

1 small jar pimentos

½ onion, chopped

1 cup celery, chopped

1 can cream of mushroom soup

1 can tomato soup

1 Tbsp. Worcestershire sauce

1 small box Velveeta cheese, finely chopped

Oil

Directions:

Stew chicken and debone. Cook spaghetti in chicken broth. Add 1 Tbsp. oil to skillet and sauté onion and celery. Drain spaghetti and add chicken, onion, celery, mushroom soup, tomato

soup and cheese.   Salt and pepper to taste.
Simmer 20 minutes, until cheese is melted.

Easy Chicken and Rice

Ingredients:

4 chicken breast

1 ½ cups rice

2 cups chicken broth

1 tsp salt

1 Tbsp. butter

Directions:

Place rice in bottom of 9" x 13" dish. Add salt, butter and chicken broth. Spread evenly in dish. Place chicken in dish. Cover and bake at 350 degrees for 1 hour and 10 minutes, until chicken is white all the way through.

Hot Chicken Salad

Ingredients:

2 cups chicken, cooked and chopped

1 can cream of chicken soup

2 cups celery, chopped

½ cup toasted almonds, chopped

1 tsp salt

¼ tsp pepper

1 Tbsp. lemon juice

½ cup mayonnaise

3 hard-boiled eggs, chopped

½ cup onion, chopped

1 cup potato chips, crushed

Directions:

Boil chicken and chop. Combine chicken with cream of chicken soup, celery, almonds, salt, pepper, lemon juice, mayonnaise, eggs and onion. Pour mixture into 9" x 13" baking dish. Sprinkle potato chips on top. Bake at 450 degrees for 15 minutes.

Spanish Pork Chops

Ingredients:

6 pork chops, trimmed

¾ cup rice

1 – 8 oz. tomato juice or sauce

1 tsp salt

1 onion, chopped

1 bell pepper, chopped

1 cup water

Directions:

Place pork chops in oven safe skillet. Place rice over pork chops, sprinkle with salt and pepper. Add onions and bell pepper. Mix tomato juice/sauce with water. Pour over all ingredients and mix. Cover and bake at 350 degrees for 45 minutes to 1 hour. Add more water during baking, if needed.

Mexican Salad

Ingredients:

1 small bag Fritos

1 head lettuce

2 tomatoes, chopped

1 can pinto or ranch beans

1 onion chopped

1 lb. cheddar cheese, grated

¾ bottle Catalina dressing

Directions:

Mix all ingredients except Fritos. Add Fritos just before serving.

Noodle Meat Dish

Ingredients;

1 ½ lb. ground beef

1 medium onion, chopped

1 can cream of mushroom soup

1 can Rotel tomatoes

1 soup can milk

4 oz. cheddar cheese, shredded

8 oz. egg noodles

Directions:

Cooked egg noodles and drain. Brown ground beef with onions, drain. Add mushroom soup, Rotel tomatoes, milk and cheese. In 9" x 13" pan layer ½ noodles, meat and sauce. Repeat. Bake at 350 **degrees for 30 minutes.**

Corn Moussaka

Ingredients:

1 – 17 oz. whole kernel corn, drained

1 ½ lbs. ground beef

1 Tbsp. flour

8 oz. tomato sauce

½ tsp garlic salt

½ tsp cinnamon

2 eggs, beaten

1 ½ cup cottage cheese, drained

¼ cup parmesan cheese

4 oz. mozzarella cheese, shredded

Directions:

Spread corn in ungreased 9" x 13" baking dish. In medium skillet brown ground beef, drain. Add flour, cook and stir for 1 minute. Stir in tomato sauce, garlic salt and cinnamon; pour over corn. Bake at 350 degrees for 15 minutes.

Meanwhile, combine eggs and cottage cheese. Spread over meat mixture. Top with parmesan and mozzarella cheeses. Return to oven for 15 minutes.

Mexican Casserole

Ingredients:

1 - 8 oz. package of nacho cheese Doritos

2 lbs. ground beef

1 – 15 oz. ranch beans

1 can cream of chicken or cream of mushroom soup

1 can Rotel tomatoes

Cheddar cheese, grated

Directions:

Layer in 9" x 13" dish in order listed. Completely cover with cheese. Bake at 350 degrees for 30 minutes.

Chicken Noodle Soup

Ingredients:

1 chicken

6 cups water

1 medium onion

2 tsp salt

¼ tsp pepper

1 bay leaf

1 ½ cups egg noodles

1 cup carrots, chopped

1 cup celery, chopped

2 Tbsp. fresh parsley or 2 tsp dried

Directions:

In large pot combine chicken, water, onion, salt, pepper and bay leaf and bring to boil, reduce heat and simmer, covered, for 2 hours or until chicken is tender.

Remove chicken from bones and chop. Skim fat from broth and discard. Bring broth to boil again and add noodles, carrots and celery; reduce heat and simmer for 8 minutes or until noodles are al dente. Stir in chicken and parsley and heat through.

Bomber Sandwiches

Ingredients:

5 - 6 lb. roast

2 bell peppers

2 onions

8 beef bouillon cubes

2 tsp seasoning salt

1 tsp garlic salt

1 Tbsp. Italian seasoning

½ stick butter (optional)

½ tsp black pepper

Hot peppers or giardiniera

Bomber buns or Kaiser rolls

Mozzarella cheese

Directions:

Place roast in roasting pan and fill the pan half way with water. Add bell peppers, onions, bouillon cubes, seasoning salt, garlic powder, Italian seasoning, butter, and black pepper. Place in 350 degree oven for 3 to 4 hours. Check occasionally. Add water, if necessary, to keep water level at half full.

When the roast is done, remove from oven and slice thin. Place the sliced meat back into the roasting pan of juices.

Serve on buns with hot peppers, mozzarella cheese and the juice dip.

Vegetable Soup

Ingredients:

1 Tbsp. oil

½ cup onion, chopped

2 cloves garlic, minced

1 – 16 oz. can diced tomatoes

1 cup chicken broth

1 cup carrots, sliced

1 cup celery, sliced

¼ cup fresh parsley

1 tsp basil, crushed

¼ tsp salt

⅛ tsp black pepper

1 cup frozen lima beans

½ cup water

Directions:

Heat oil in medium saucepan over medium-high heat. Add onion and garlic and cook 3 minutes or until soft. Add tomatoes, chicken broth, carrots, celery, parsley, basil, salt and pepper; bring to boil. Reduce heat and simmer for 20 minutes, covered. Reduce heat. Add lima beans and bring to boil. Reduce heat and simmer for 20 minutes, until beans are tender. 4 servings

Tuna Pasta Bake

Ingredients:

4 tsp oil

1 cup onion

2 clove garlic, minced

2 small can tomato sauce

1 tsp oregano

8 oz. spaghetti (4 cups cooked)

1 – 14 oz. can tuna in water, drained

1 cup cooked sweet peas

2 cup cottage cheese

2 egg, slightly beaten

1/2 tsp black pepper

3 Tbsp. wheat germ or bread crumbs

Directions:

Heat oil in small saucepan over medium-high heat and cook onion and garlic for 3 minutes. Add tomato sauce and oregano, bring to boil. Reduce heat and cover. Simmer about 15 minutes, stirring occasionally.

Meanwhile, cook spaghetti to al dente. Drain, place in medium bowl and add tuna and peas; toss well.

In small bowl combine cottage cheese, egg and pepper. Pour over spaghetti; mix well. Grease 9" x 13" baking dish. Pour spaghetti mixture in dish and pour sauce over. Bake 30 minutes, until hot and bubbly.

Oven Baked Fried Chicken

Ingredients:

1 chicken or preferred pieces

1 cup plain yogurt

3 ½ cups ice water

1 cup Italian bread crumbs

1 cup flour

1 Tbsp. Old Bay seasoning

½ tsp garlic powder

½ tsp Cajun seasoning

¼ tsp black pepper

¼ tsp cayenne pepper

½ tsp thyme

½ tsp basil

½ tsp oregano

Directions:

Soak chicken in ice water for 30 minutes. Combine bread crumbs, flour, Old Bay, garlic powder, Cajun seasoning, pepper, cayenne pepper, thyme, basil and oregano in Ziploc bag and mix thoroughly.
Put yogurt in bowl. Roll chicken in yogurt, then place in bag of bread crumb mixture and coat with dry ingredients.

Place on greased baking sheet and spray with cooking spray. Bake in 400 degree oven on bottom shelf for 1 hour, turning pieces every 15 to 20 minutes.

Oven Baked Fried Catfish

Ingredients:

4 catfish fillets

¼ cup cornmeal

1 tsp thyme

1 tsp basil

½ tsp garlic powder

½ tsp lemon pepper

4 tsp blackening seasoning

½ tsp paprika

Directions:

Mix cornmeal, thyme and basil in Ziploc bag or pie plate, mix well. Sprinkle $^1/_8$ tsp garlic powder, $^1/_8$ tsp lemon pepper and 1 tsp blackening seasoning on each catfish fillet. Place fillets in bag of cornmeal mixture or on pie plate and coat well. Place on greased baking sheet and spray fillets with cooking spray.

Bake in 400 degree oven for 20 minutes on bottom shelf. Reduce heat to 350 degrees and bake for 5 more minutes or until fish flakes.

Chicken in Wine Sauce

Ingredients:

2 Tbsp. oil

4 boneless chicken breast

3 ½ cups mushrooms, sliced

¼ cup onion, chopped

2 garlic cloves, minced

½ cup dry red wine

$1/3$ cup + 1 ½ Tbsp. water

¼ tsp thyme, crushed

¼ tsp salt

$1/8$ tsp black pepper

2 tsp flour

2 Tbsp. fresh parsley

Directions:

In large skillet heat oil and brown chicken. Remove from skillet. Add mushrooms, onion and garlic and cook 5 minutes or until tender. Return chicken to skillet. Add red wine, $^1/_3$ cup water, thyme, salt and pepper; bring to boil. Reduce heat and cover. Simmer 20 minutes or until chicken is tender, turning once. Transfer chicken to serving platter and keep warm.

In small bowl, combine flour and 1 ½ Tbsp. water. Add to skillet and cook 1 minute, stirring constantly. Stir in parsley. Spoon sauce over chicken.

Jambalaya

Ingredients:

1 lb. smoked sausage

2 Tbsp. oil

1 ½ cups onion, chopped

½ cup green onion

½ cup bell pepper, chopped

¼ cup fresh parsley

1 small can tomato sauce

1 tsp garlic, minced

¼ tsp mint, crushed

1 cup dry white wine

1 ½ cup rice

Salt to taste

Louisiana hot sauce to taste

Directions:

Heat oil in large skillet over medium-high heat and sauté onions, green onions, bell pepper and parsley until onions are tender. Add tomato sauce, garlic, mint and wine; mix well. Add rice, salt, hot sauce, smoked sausage and enough water to cover the rice by 1 inch. Cook until most of the juice is gone. Reduce heat to low, cover and simmer for 1 hour. Do not lift the lid until near end of cooking time.

Cajun Stew

Ingredients:

2 lbs. ground beef or finely chopped roast

1 Tbsp. oil

1 head cabbage, cut in half and sliced

2 can Ranch style bean

2 cans Rotel tomatoes

1 can diced tomatoes

2 cloves garlic, minced

1 Tbsp. cayenne pepper

2 tsp cumin

Salt and pepper to taste

Directions:

Cook ground beef or roast and chopped finely. In large pot, heat oil. Place rest of ingredients in pot and stir well. May adjust seasoning to taste.

Italian Delight

Ingredients:

½ lb. macaroni

2 lbs. ground beef

3 medium onions, chopped

1 bell pepper, minced

1 clove garlic, minced

4 Tbsp. butter

4 small cans tomato sauce

1 can corn

3 – 3 oz. cans mushrooms, sliced with liquid

1 Tbsp. brown sugar

1 Tbsp. Worcestershire sauce

2 Tbsp. chili powder

2 tsp salt

¼ tsp black pepper

1 cup cheddar cheese, shredded

Directions:

Cook macaroni to al dente; drain. Melt butter in skillet and brown meat with onion, bell pepper and garlic. Transfer to deep 9" x 13" casserole dish. Stir in all ingredients and mix well. Bake at 350 degrees, covered, for 2 hours or until it bubbles.

Pork Tenderloin with Wild Huckleberry, Elderberry or Blueberry Sauce

Ingredients:

Pork tenderloin

3 Tbsp. olive oil

2 Tbsp. fresh rosemary, finely chopped or 2 tsp dried

2 Tbsp. fresh thyme, finely chopped or 2 tsp dried

2 Tbsp. fresh sage, finely chopped or 2 tsp dried

1 Tbsp. coarse salt

1 tsp black pepper

2 cups, huckleberries, elderberries, or blueberries

1/3 cup sugar

2 Tbsp. raspberry vinegar

¼ cup white wine or chicken broth

Directions:

Lightly rub pork with olive oil. Combine herbs, salt and pepper in plate. Roll the pork loin in the mixture and rub in.

In saucepan, combine berries, sugar, vinegar and wine/broth and bring to boil. Lower the heat and simmer until slightly thickened.

In heavy skillet over medium high heat, sauté the pork on all side until golden brown. Place in the oven for 12 to 15 minutes or until internal temperature is 150. May skip these steps and cook on grill until 150 internal temperature.

Transfer to serving platter and spoon sauce over.

Super Easy Shepherd's Pie

Ingredients:

1 lb. ground beef

1 can tomato soup

1 can green beans

5 potatoes

Directions:

Boil potatoes, mash and season with salt and pepper. Brown ground beef. Mix green beans, tomato soup and ground beef; pour in 9" x 13" dish. Top with mashed potatoes. Bake at 350 degrees for 30 minutes. May top with grated cheddar, if you desire.

Buffalo Chicken Pasta

Ingredients:

2 cups penne pasta, uncooked

1 – 8 oz. cream cheese

¾ cup ranch dressing

1/3 cup hot wing sauce

2 cups cooked chicken, shredded

1 ½ cup mozzarella cheese

½ cup cheddar cheese

Green onions, chopped

Directions:

Cook pasta until al dente, drain. Stir together cream cheese, ranch and wing sauce until creamy. Add chicken, ½ cup mozzarella and pasta, mix well. Pour into 8" casserole dish. Combine remaining cheeses and sprinkle over top of mixture.

Bake at 375 degrees for 20 minutes or until cheese is melted. Sprinkle with chopped onion. Drizzle with wing sauce and ranch dressing.

Cowgirl Stew

Ingredients:

2 Tbsp. oil

2 lbs. ground beef
3 cups water

1 – 16 oz. pkg. frozen corn
1 – 15 oz. can tomatoes
1 can ranch beans
6 potatoes, peeled and cubed
1 onion, chopped
1 bell pepper, chopped
¼ cup celery, chopped
2 Tbsp. chili powder
¼ tsp sugar
¼ tsp garlic powder
Salt and black pepper to taste

Directions:

Heat oil in large pot over medium heat. Cook ground beef until brown. Add rest of ingredients to pot. Cover and bring to boil. Reduce heat and simmer until potatoes are tender...about 1 hour.

185

Goulash

Ingredients:

2 lbs. ground beef

3 tsp garlic, minced

1 onion, diced

2 ½ cups water

½ cup beef broth

1/3 cup olive oil

2 – 15 oz. cans tomato sauce

2 – 15 oz. cans tomatoes

1 Tbsp. Italian seasoning

1 Tbsp. Adobo seasoning

3 bay leaves

1 Tbsp. seasoned salt

½ Tbsp. black pepper

2 cups elbow macaroni, uncooked

1 cup mozzarella cheese, shredded (optional)

½ cup cheddar cheese, shredded (optional)
Directions:

In large pot sauté ground beef until half-cooked. Add garlic, onions and olive oil and finish cooking. Add water, broth, tomato sauce, tomatoes, Italian seasoning, bay leaves, seasoned salt, pepper and adobo seasoning. Mix well. Lower heat and cover; simmer for 20 minutes, stirring occasionally. Add elbow macaroni and stir well. Cover and simmer for 30 minutes. Once cooked remove bay leaves. If desired, add cheeses and mix until combined.

Baked Chicken Thighs

Ingredients:

8 chicken thighs

2 Tbsp. butter

2 cloves garlic, chopped

1 cup Dijon mustard

½ tsp cayenne, divided

1 1 /2 cups panko bread crumbs

¾ cup Parmesan, grated

¼ cup fresh chives or parsley

2 tsp paprika

Salt

Directions:

Melt butter; add garlic, ¼ tsp cayenne and mustard, whisk together.

In another bowl, combine bread crumbs, Parmesan, chives/parsley, paprika and ¼ tsp cayenne.

Salt thighs. Dip chicken in mustard mixture and roll in breadcrumbs. Place on lightly grease baking sheet. Bake at 425 degrees for 40 minutes. \4\

Mexican Squash and Ground Beef Casserole

Ingredients:

1 lb. ground beef

1 Tbsp. oil

3 cups yellow squash, sliced

1 small onion, sliced

1 clove garlic, minced

1 – 14 oz. can diced tomatoes

1 tsp chili powder

1 tsp cumin

1 tsp smoked paprika

Salt and pepper to taste

1 cup cheddar cheese, shredded

Directions:

In large skillet cook ground beef and drain. Heat oil in medium skillet over medium heat and sauté squash, onion and garlic until tender. Add ground beef, tomatoes, chili powder, cumin, paprika, salt and pepper, mix well.

Pour into 9" x 13" baking dish and bake at 400 degrees for 15 minutes.

Chicken Chili with Black Beans

Ingredients:

3 boneless, skinless chicken breast, cubed

2 medium sweet red peppers, chopped

1 large onion, chopped

3 Tbsp. olive oil

1 can chopped green chiles

4 cloves garlic, minced

2 Tbsp. chili powder

2 tsp ground cumin

1 tsp ground coriander

2 – 15 oz. cans black beans, drained and rinsed

1 - 28 oz. can Italian stewed tomatoes, diced

1 cup chicken broth or beer

½ to 1 cup water

Directions:

In large pot, sauté chicken, red peppers and onion in oil until chicken is cooked. Add the green chiles, garlic, chili powder, cumin and coriander; cook 1 minute longer. Stir in the beans, tomatoes, broth/beer and ½ cup water; bring to boil. Reduce and simmer, uncovered for 15 minutes, stirring often and adding water, as necessary.

Sweet Potato Ham Corn Chowder

Ingredients:

1 ½ tsp olive oil

1 large onion, chopped

1 cup carrots, diced

1 cup celery, diced

1 cup bell pepper, chopped

3 cloves garlic, minced

3 ¾ cup chicken broth

3 cups sweet potato, peeled and diced

1 tsp basil

½ tsp thyme

Salt and black pepper to taste

5 Tbsp. unsalted butter, sliced

1/3 cup flour

3 cups milk

1 ½ cup ham, diced

1 ½ cups corn

½ cup cheddar cheese, shredded; plus more for serving

3 Tbsp. parsley, chopped

Directions:

Heat olive oil in large pot over medium high heat. Add onions, carrots and celery; sauté for 4 minutes. Add bell pepper and garlic and sauté 1 minute longer. Add chicken broth, sweet potatoes, basil, thyme, salt and pepper.

Bring mixture to boil, then reduce heat to medium low and simmer until potatoes and vegetables are tender, 15 to 20 minutes.

Melt butter in saucepan over medium heat. Add flour and cook, whisking constantly, for 1 minute.

Stir ham and corn into soup and heat through, about 2 minutes. Stir milk mixture into soup. Stir in cheddar cheese and parsley.

Slaw Burger

Ingredients:

2 cups ham, cooked and chopped

2 cups brisket, cooked and chopped

Coleslaw

Barbeque sauce

Hamburger buns

Directions:

Mix ham and brisket together. Put on bun. Top with coleslaw and barbeque sauce.

Broccoli and Cheddar Frittata

Ingredients:

8 large eggs

2 tsp olive oil

1 small red onion, sliced

2 cups cooked broccoli, chopped

¼ tsp salt

Black pepper to taste

½ cup extra sharp Cheddar cheese

Directions:

Separate 4 eggs; set whites aside and discard yolks or save for later use. Add the 4 whole eggs and 2 tablespoons water to the whites and whisk well.

In ovenproof skillet, heat oil over medium heat. Add the onion and cook until soft. Add the broccoli and cook for 2 minutes. Season with salt and pepper. Pour the egg mixture into the skillet and cover vegetables evenly...do not stir. Reduce the heat to medium low, cover and let cook until eggs have set around the edges. Sprinkle with cheese. Place skillet in oven, under broiler, until surface is set and it is golden brown...1 to 2 minutes.

Pepperoni Pizza Crescent Rolls

Ingredients:

1 can crescent rolls

32 slices pepperoni

4 pieces mozzarella string cheese, cut in half

Garlic powder

Italian seasoning

Pizza sauce

Directions:

Preheat the oven to 375 degrees. Unroll the crescent rolls into triangles. Top each crescent roll with 4 pieces of pepperoni, then a piece of string cheese; roll up (tuck the corners to keep all the cheese from oozing out) and place on a baking sheet. Dust tops with garlic powder and Italian seasoning; bake for 20 to 23 minutes, or until golden brown. Serve with your favorite pizza sauce for dipping.

Parmesan Garlic Mushroom Chicken

Ingredients:

4 boneless, skinless chicken breast, thinly sliced

2 Tbsp. olive oil

8 oz. sliced mushrooms

¼ cup butter

2 cloves garlic

1 Tbsp. flour

½ cup chicken broth

1 cup heavy cream or half and half

½ cup parmesan cheese, grated

½ tsp garlic powder

¼ tsp pepper

½ tsp salt

1 cup spinach, chopped

Pasta

Directions:

In a large skillet, heat oil over medium high heat for 3 – 5 minutes. Season chicken and cook on each side or until brown on each side. Set chicken aside. Add the sliced mushrooms and cook for a few minutes, until tender. Remove and set aside

Add butter to skillet and melt. Add garlic and cook until tender. Whisk in the flour and cook until thickened. Whisk in chicken broth, heavy cream/half and half, parmesan cheese, garlic powder, salt and pepper. Add the spinach and let simmer until it starts to thicken and spinach wilts. Add the chicken and mushroom back to the sauce and serve over pasta.

Pesto Pasta Chicken

Ingredients:

16 oz. bow-tie pasta

1 tsp olive oil, plus $^2/_3$ cup

4 cloves garlic, minced

Salt and pepper to taste

2 boneless chicken breasts, chopped

Crushed red pepper flakes, to taste

1/3 cup oil packed sun-dried tomatoes, drained and cut into strips

2 cups packed fresh basil leaves

¼ cup pine nuts

½ cup Pecorino Romano or Parmesan cheese, grated

Directions:

Cook pasta according to package directions. Heat teaspoon oil in large skillet over medium heat. Sauté 2 cloves garlic until tender. Stir in chicken; season with red pepper flakes. Cook until chicken is browned.

Combine basil, 2 cloves garlic and pine nuts in food processor and pulse until coarsely chopped. Add ½ cup of oil and process until smooth. Season with salt and pepper. Transfer to bowl and stir in cheese

In large bowl combine pasta, chicken, sun-dried tomatoes and pesto. Toss to coat.

Caribbean Pulled Pork Sandwich

Ingredients:

1 lg. pulled pork

1 cup chicken broth

1 – 2 Tbsp. dry pork rub

6 Pretzel buns or hamburger buns

1 stick butter, softened

6 eggs

Salt and pepper, to taste

6 slices cheddar cheese

1 ¼ cup mango peach salsa

Dry Rub:

1 Tbsp. cumin

1 Tbsp. garlic powder

1 Tbsp. onion powder

1 Tbsp. chili powder

1 Tbsp. cayenne pepper

1 Tbsp. salt

1 Tbsp. black pepper

1 Tbsp. paprika

½ cup brown sugar

Directions:

In large skillet over medium heat add pulled pork, broth and dry rub; mix well. Simmer over medium low heat until heated through.

Place open pretzel buns, inside facing up, on baking sheet. Generously apply butter and broil in the oven until golden and toasted. Set aside

Season eggs and cook in butter until over medium...runny yolk.

Place bun on plate and top with layers of cheddar cheese, pulled pork, fried egg and salsa.

Ham & Cheese Quiche

Ingredients:

3 eggs, beaten

¾ cup milk

Salt and pepper, to taste

1 cup ham, chopped

1 cup cheddar cheese, shredded

1 – 9" pie crust

Directions:

Beat eggs with milk, salt and pepper in bowl. Add ham and cheese. Pour into pie crust and bake at 350 degrees for 45 minutes.

Mexican Cornbread Casserole

Ingredients:

1 pkg. corn bread mix

1 egg

1/3 cup milk

¾ cup frozen corn, divided

½ lb. ground beef

1 can Rotel tomatoes, drained

1 – 8 oz. can tomato sauce

½ tsp cumin

1 cup Mexican cheese blend or cheddar cheese, shredded

Directions:

Stir together corn bread mix, egg, milk and half of corn in bowl. Pour into 8" x 8" baking dish.

Meanwhile, cook beef in medium skillet over medium high heat, drain. Stir in drained Rotel tomatoes, tomato sauce, remaining corn and cumin. Pour mixture over top of batter. Top with cheese. Bake in 375 degree oven for 15 – 20 minutes or until lightly browned and corn bread is done.

Grilled Pork Chops with Honey-Jalapeno Marinade

Ingredients:

½ cup olive oil

1 tsp lemon zest

¼ cup lemon juice

¼ cup honey

6 cloves garlic, minced

1 jalapeno pepper, seeded and minced

1 tsp thyme

1 tsp paprika

1 tsp salt

½ tsp black pepper

2 lbs. bone-in pork chops

Directions:

In a large Ziploc bag, combine oil, lemon zest, lemon juice, honey, garlic, jalapeno, thyme, paprika, 1 teaspoon salt and ½ teaspoon pepper.

Add pork chops and rub until evenly coated. Marinade for up to 2 hours at room temperature, turning occasionally, or in the refrigerator overnight. If refrigerated, bring to room temperature before cooking.

Preheat grill and grill chops over medium high heat until well browned...3 to 4 minutes. Transfer to a medium low heat part of the grill and cover. Cook until 155 degrees internal temperature.

Egg Pasta Frittata

Ingredients:

12 oz. box fettuccini pasta

2 Tbsp. olive oil

2 Tbsp. butter

1 cup heavy cream

1 cup Parmesan, grated

½ tsp nutmeg

Salt and black pepper, to taste

¼ cup flat-leaf parsley, chopped

12 large eggs, beaten

Directions:

Cook pasta according to package directions. Add oil and butter to oven safe skillet; melt together. Add cream and reduce for about 3 minutes. Add cheese, nutmeg, salt and pepper. Toss sauce with cooked pasta to coat. Add parsley and beaten eggs the skillet; stir to combine. Cook until eggs begin to set around edges. Remove from heat and bake in 425 degree oven for 10 minutes or until golden.

Cowboy Beans
(Frijoles Charros)

Ingredients:

2 lbs. dried pinto beans, cooked

1 large onion

1 bell pepper, chopped

1 large can tomatoes, diced

6 Serrano chiles

4 cloves garlic, minced

1 bunch cilantro, chopped

10 jalapenos, chopped

1 Tbsp. chili powder

2 tsp Mexican oregano

2 tsp cumin

2 tsp paprika

2 bay leaves

2 tsp cinnamon

1 tsp thyme

¼ cup brown sugar

1 Tbsp. yellow mustard

8 oz. bacon

15 oz. Mexican-style chorizo or ground beef

Directions:

Cooked beans according to package directions. Slice bacon into small chunks and cook over medium heat until crisp. Add chorizo/ground beef and cook.
Add onion, serrano peppers and garlic to bacon and cook until tender. Add tomatoes.

Add chorizo/ground beef mixture to beans. Bring to boil. Skim fat off the top. Simmer for 15 minutes. Add cilantro, to taste. Cook for 5 minutes.

Red Beans and Rice

Ingredients:

1 lb. dry kidney beans

¼ cup olive oil

1 large onion, chopped

1 bell pepper, chopped

2 Tbsp. garlic, minced

2 stalks celery, chopped

10 cups water, divided

2 bay leaves

½ tsp cayenne pepper

1 tsp thyme

¼ tsp sage

1 Tbsp. dried parsley or 3 Tbsp. fresh

1 tsp Cajun seasoning

1 lb. andouille sausage, sliced

2 cups rice

Directions:

Rinse beans and soak overnight in large pot. In skillet, heat oil over medium heat. Add onion, bell pepper, garlic and celery and cook until tender. Rinse beans and add 6 cups of water. Stir in cooked vegetables. Add bay leaves, cayenne pepper, thyme, sage, parsley and Cajun seasoning. Bring to boil and then reduce heat to medium low and simmer for 2 ½ hours. Stir in sausage and continue to simmer for 30 minutes.

Meanwhile, prepare rice according to package directions. Serve beans over rice.

Texas Chili

Ingredients:

2 pounds of ground chuck

1 large onion, chopped

28 ounces Rotel tomatoes

2 cloves garlic

16 oz. tomato sauce

½ cup chili powder (less if you can't take much heat)

2 tsp cumin

1 tsp cayenne pepper

2 cups beans (if desired)

2 cups water

Cheddar cheese, shredded

Directions:

Brown the meat with onion. Add the remaining ingredients. Simmer for 1 ½ hours. Serve hot with grated cheddar cheese.

Pork and Rice Skillet

Ingredients:

2 Tbsp. olive oil

1 lb. boneless pork chops, approx. 3 cups

½ onion, diced

2 cloves garlic, minced

1 cup rice

1 Tbsp. Italian seasoning

1 cup frozen peas and carrots

2 cups chicken broth

½ cup sour cream

1 ½ cup cheddar cheese, shredded

Directions:

Heat oil in large skillet over medium heat. Sauté pork with garlic and onions until pork is browned and onions tender. Add rice, Italian seasoning, frozen peas and carrots and chicken broth, mix well. Bring to boil. Cover and reduce heat to simmer for 18 minutes, stirring occasionally.

Stir in the sour cream and ½ cup cheese, mix well. Top with remaining cheese. Cover and cook for 2 to 3 minutes or until cheese melts.

Pozole (Po-zo-là)

<u>Ingredients</u>:

1 large head garlic

12 cups water

4 cups chicken broth

4 pounds country style ribs

1 tsp dried Mexican oregano

2 oz. dried New Mexico/Anaheim/Hatch chiles

1 ½ cups boiling water

¼ large white onion

3 tsp salt

2 – 30 oz. cans white hominy

8 corn tortillas

½ cup oil

Directions:

Peel garlic and reserve 2 cloves for chili sauce. Slice remaining garlic. In a 7 – 8 quart pot, bring water and broth to a boil with sliced garlic and pork. Skim fat from surface and add oregano. Gently simmer the pork, uncovered, until tender…about 1 ½ hours.

While pork is simmering, remove stems from chiles. In a bowl, combine chiles with boiling water. Soak chiles, turning them occasionally, for 30 minutes. Cut onion into large pieces and in a blender, puree with chiles, soaking liquid, remaining garlic and 2 teaspoons salt, until smooth.

Shred pork, using 2 forks. Drain and rinse hominy. Return pork to broth, add chili sauce, hominy and remaining teaspoon of salt. Simmer 30 minutes.

While pozole is simmering, cut tortillas in thin strips. Heat ½ inch oil in skillet and fry tortilla strips until golden. Drain on paper towel.

Indian Tacos

Ingredients:

1 lbs. pinto beans, cooked

2 lbs. ground beef

1 pkg. taco seasoning

2 tomatoes

2 onions, chopped

1 head of lettuce, chopped

4 cups cheddar cheese, shredded

Picante sauce

4 cups flour

2 cups water

2 cups oil

Directions:

Cook beans. Brown ground beef in skillet; add taco seasoning and set aside. Prepare fry bread: Mix flour and water and knead to make stiff dough. Knead on floured board. Heat oil in iron skillet until hot. Pinch off 3" balls of dough, pat out to circle ½" thick and drop in hot oil. Brown on both sides. Layer fry bread, beans, meat, onions, lettuce, tomatoes and cheese. Pour picante sauce on. Bread is also good with honey.

Texas Hash

Ingredients:

2 Tbsp. olive oil

1 lb. ground beef

1 cup onions, diced

1 cup bell pepper, diced

1 Tbsp. garlic, minced

½ tsp dry mustard

2 tsp chili powder

2 tsp salt

¼ tsp black pepper

½ cup rice

2 Tbsp. tomato paste

1 – 14.5 oz. can diced tomatoes

1 cup water

1 tsp Worcestershire sauce

1 cup cheddar cheese, shredded (optional)

Directions:

Heat oil over medium-high heat. Add ground beef, onion, bell peppers, garlic, salt and pepper and cook until meat is browned. Add rice and cook for 2 minutes. Add tomato paste and cook for 1 minute. Add canned tomatoes, water and Worcestershire sauce. Stir, cover and simmer for 20 minutes. If cheese is used, sprinkle on during last few minutes of cooking.

Parmesan Orzo

Ingredients:

$2/3$ cup orzo pasta

1 Tbsp. butter

2 Tbsp. cream or milk

¼ cup Parmesan cheese, shredded

Salt and black pepper to taste

Directions:

Cook orzo pasta according to package directions. Drain and add butter until melted. Stir in milk/cream, cheese, salt and pepper.

Squash Casserole

Ingredients:

4 lbs. yellow squash, sliced

1 onion, finely chopped

1 cup cheddar cheese, shredded

1 cup mayonnaise

2 Tbsp. fresh basil or 2 tsp dried

1 tsp garlic salt

1 tsp black pepper

2 large eggs, slightly beaten

2 cups breadcrumbs, divided

1 ¼ cup Parmesan cheese, shredded, divided

2 Tbsp. butter, melted

½ cup French fried onions, crushed

Directions:

Cook squash and onion is boiling water for 8 minutes or until tender, drain. Combine squash, onion, cheese, mayonnaise, basil, salt, pepper, eggs, 1 cup bread crumbs and Parmesan, mix well. Pour into lightly greased 9" x 13" baking dish.

Stir together butter, fried onion, 1 cup bread crumbs and Parmesan cheese. Spring over squash mixture. Bake at 350 degrees for 35 to 40 minutes.

Broccoli Cauliflower Salad

Ingredients:

1 - 2 heads of broccoli

1 head cauliflower

1 small can chopped black olives

Ranch dressing

Directions:

Chop broccoli and cauliflower. Combine broccoli, cauliflower and olives. Add enough ranch dressing to coat.

Sautéed Zucchini

Ingredients:

2 Tbsp. olive oil

1 clove garlic, crushed

1 fresh ginger root, sliced or ½ tsp ground ginger

2 – 3 small unpeeled zucchini, ½" slices

¼ cup white wine

½ tsp salt

$1/_8$ tsp pepper

1 cup hot chicken broth

Directions:

Pour oil into pan and preheat. Add garlic and ginger and stir fry until garlic is brown, about 5 minutes. Add zucchini, wine, salt and pepper and stir fry for 2 minutes. Add chicken broth and reduce heat to medium low, cover and simmer for 3 to 4 minutes. Zucchini should be tender, but slightly crunchy toward the out edges. Serve immediately.

Baked Beans

Ingredients:

8 slices bacon, cut in half

1 onion, small diced

½ bell pepper, small diced

3 – 28 oz. cans pork and beans

¾ cup barbecue sauce

½ cup brown sugar

¼ cup cider vinegar

2 tsp dry mustard

Directions:

In large pot, fry bacon until partially cooked; drain on paper towels. Add onions and peppers to drippings and sauté until tender. Add beans and remain ingredients; bring to simmer. Pour into greased 9" x 13" pan. Top with bacon and bake in 325 degree oven, on lower-middle rack, until bubbly and sauce is thick...about 2 hours.

Texas Caviar

Ingredients:

½ onion, chopped

1 bell pepper, chopped

1 bunch green onions, chopped

2 jalapeno peppers, chopped

1 Tbsp. garlic, minced

1 pint cherry tomatoes, quartered

1 – 8 oz. bottle zesty Italian dressing

1 – 15 oz. can black beans, drained

1 – 15 oz. can black-eyed peas, drained

½ tsp ground coriander

1 bunch fresh cilantro, chopped

Directions:

Mix all ingredients, except cilantro, in large bowl. Refrigerate for 2 hours. Toss with desired amount of cilantro.

Harvard Beets

Ingredients:

¾ cup sugar

4 tsp corn starch

$^1/_3$ cup water

2 – 15 oz. cans sliced beets, drained

3 Tbsp. butter

¼ tsp salt

¼ tsp black pepper

Directions:

In saucepan, combine sugar, cornstarch, vinegar and water. Bring to boil and cook for 5 minutes, until thickened. Add the beets and simmer for 30 minutes over low heat. Stir in butter, salt and pepper. Serve warm or cold.

Louisiana-Style Picadillo

Ingredients:

2 cups instant rice

2 ½ cups water

1 lb. ground beef

½ cup onion, chopped

2 cloves garlic, minced

2 cups sliced okra (fresh or 10 oz. frozen)

½ tsp salt

½ tsp cayenne pepper

¼ tsp black pepper

1 – 15 oz. can kidney beans, drained and rinsed

1 – 14.5 can Rotel tomatoes

Directions:

Cook rice in 2 cups water, as directed...cover and keep warm. In large skillet, cook ground beef, onion and garlic; drain. Stir in remaining water and all ingredients, except rice. Cover and simmer 10 minutes or until okra is tender, stirring occasionally. Serve over rice; sprinkle with green onions.

Macaroni and Cheese

Ingredients:

1 Tbsp. butter

2 cups elbow macaroni

2 cups extra sharp cheddar cheese, shredded

2 cups milk

2 large eggs, lightly beaten

Salt and pepper to taste

Directions:

Cook macaroni until tender. In large bowl, combine all ingredients. Pour into buttered 9" x 13" baking dish. Bake at 350 degrees for 30 minutes.

Potato Salad

Ingredients:

5 potatoes, peeled and boiled

1 cup dill pickles, chopped

½ onion, chopped

¼ tsp celery seed

½ cup mayonnaise

¼ cup mustard

Directions:

Mash potatoes and add pickles, onion and celery seed. Add mayonnaise and mustard. Add more or less mustard and mayonnaise for desired consistency and taste.

Cucumber Salad

Ingredients:

1 cup sugar

½ cup vinegar

1 tsp salt

½ tsp celery seed

½ cup sliced red onions

2 - 3 quartered tomatoes

Directions:

Mix all ingredients and refrigerate for 3 hours.

Sweet Potato Bake

Ingredients:

3 cups sweet potatoes

1 cup sugar

½ cup butter, melted

2 eggs, beaten

Directions:

Boil and mash potatoes. Combine all ingredients and put in 9" x 13" casserole dish.

Topping

Ingredients:

1 cup brown sugar

½ cup flour

$^1/_3$ butter, melted

1 cup nuts, chopped

Directions:

Mix all ingredients and sprinkle over potatoes. Bake at 350 degrees for 30 to 40 minutes.

Spanish Rice

Ingredients:

4 slices bacon

½ onion, chopped

1 bell pepper, chopped

1 large can tomatoes, diced

1/8 tsp black pepper

Cheddar cheese, grated

1 cup instant rice

Directions:

Fry bacon and dice. Cook onion in grease until soft. Combine rice, bacon, onion, bell pepper, tomatoes and black pepper and put in a loaf pan. Sprinkled with grated cheese and bake at 350 degrees for 25 to 30 minutes.

Cornbread Dressing

Ingredients:

3 ½ cups cornbread, crumbled

3 ½ cups old white bread or biscuits, crumbled

1 onion, chopped

1 cups celery, chopped

2 tsp salt

½ tsp black pepper

2 tsp poultry seasoning

2 tsp sage

4 Tbsp. butter, melted

5 eggs, slightly beaten

2 – 3 cups chicken broth

Directions:

Sauté celery and onions until tender. Mix all ingredients together in roasting pan. Add as much broth as needed to moist all bread. Adjust seasonings according to taste. Bake in 350 degree oven for 40 to 45 minutes, until top is set and lightly browned. May add shredded chicken or turkey, if desired.

5 Cup Salad

Ingredients:

1 cup mandarin oranges

1 cup diced pineapple

1 cup shredded coconut

1 cup small marshmallows

1 cup sour cream

1 cup pecans, chopped

Directions:

Combine all ingredients except sour cream, mix well. Add sour cream and mix.

Cranberry Salad

Ingredients:

1 pkg. cherry gelatin

1 cup boiling water

1 cup sugar

1 tsp lemon juice

1 cup pineapple juice

1 cup ground uncooked cranberries

1 orange, ground

1 cup crushed pineapple, crushed

1 cup celery, chopped

1 cup apple, chopped

½ cup walnuts, chopped

Directions:

Dissolve gelatin in hot water. Add sugar, lemon juice and pineapple juice. Stir to dissolve. Chill until partially set. Add remaining ingredients. Chill.

Pineapple Casserole

Ingredients:

1 cup sugar

6 Tbsp. flour

2 cups grated cheese

2 – 20 oz. cans pineapple chunks, drained (reserve 6 Tbsp. juice)

1 cup Ritz cracker crumbs

1 stick butter, melted

Directions:

Combine sugar and flour. Gradually stir in cheese. Add pineapple chunks; mix well. Pour into greased 8" x 11" casserole dish.

Combine cracker crumbs, butter and pineapple juice. Spread on top of pineapple mixture. Bake in 350 degree oven for 25 to 30 minutes or until golden brown.

Deviled Eggs

Ingredients:

1 dozen eggs

$^2/_3$ cup mayonnaise

½ cup sweet pickle relish, drained

2 Tbsp. yellow mustard

2 tsp Worcestershire sauce

½ tsp salt

¼ - ½ tsp white pepper

6 drops hot pepper sauce

Paprika

Directions:

Boil eggs for 10 minutes. Pour off hot water and cover in ice water for 15 minutes. Peel eggs and cut in half. Remove yolks and put in bowl. Mash yolks with a fork and mix in remaining ingredients,

except paprika.   Spoon filling into egg whites.
Sprinkle with paprika.

Armadillo Eggs

Ingredients:

4 oz. cream cheese, room temperature

¼ cup cheddar cheese, shredded

1 clove garlic, minced

1 tsp cilantro, chopped

¼ tsp cumin

Salt to taste

6 medium jalapenos

2 lbs. breakfast sausage

Buttermilk dressing, for serving

Salsa, for serving

Directions:

Mix together cream cheese, cheddar cheese, garlic, cilantro and cumin, mix well. Add salt to taste.

Remove stems and seed from jalapenos. Cut in half lengthwise. Place a teaspoon of cream cheese filling in each jalapeno. Divide the sausage into 24 equal size portions and pat each into a 3 inch circle. Place a stuffed jalapeno in the center of the sausage circles. Wrap the sausage around the stuffed jalapeno until it's completely covered; form into an egg shape.

Place wrapped jalapenos on a lightly greased 9" x 13" cook sheet and bake at 375 for 15 to 20 minutes or until the sausage is cooked. If additional browning is needed, place under broiler for 2 to 5 minutes.

Salsa Verde

Ingredients:

3 cloves garlic, unpeeled

1 lb. fresh tomatillos, husked and rinsed

1 small onion, quartered

3 – 6 serrano chiles or 2 – 4 jalapenos

¼ cup cilantro

½ tsp sugar

Salt to taste

2 Tbsp. olive oil

1 cup chicken broth

2 Tbsp. lime juice

Directions:

Heat barbecue grill to medium-high. Thread garlic, tomatillos, onion quarters and chiles onto skewers separately. Grill on all sides. Approximately 9 minutes for onion, 6 minutes for chiles and tomatillos and 4 minutes for garlic.

Cool. Peel garlic. Scrape some of the burnt skin from the chiles and remove stem. Remove seeds for a milder salsa. Coarsely chop onion, chiles and garlic. Place all vegetables in a blender. Add cilantro and ½ teaspoon sugar; puree until smooth. Season to taste.

Heat oil over high heat in large saucepan and add tomatillo mixture. Stir until slightly thickened, stirring often. Add broth and 2 tablespoons lime juice. Bring to boil; reduce heat to medium and simmer until mixture measures about 2 ½ cups, about 10 minutes. Season to taste and add more sugar and lime juice if desired.

Guacamole

Ingredients:

3 ripe avocados

¾ cup Roma tomatoes, finely chopped

2 serrano or jalapeno chiles, seeded, finely chopped

3 heaping Tbsp. onion, finely chopped

3 Tbsp. cilantro, chopped

¾ tsp salt

Directions:

Remove rind from avocados. Mash avocados with fork. Add rest of ingredients and mix well

Best method

Add chopped onion, chiles, cilantro and salt to molcajete (rough stone mortar and pestle). Grind to smooth paste. Add avocados and grind until slightly chunky. Add tomatoes and mix well.

Sausage Egg and Cheese Turnovers

Ingredients:

1 ½ lb. sausage
4 eggs
1 Tbsp. butter
½ cup cheddar cheese, shredded
2 can biscuits

Directions:

Cook sausage, drain. Beat eggs. Place skillet over medium heat and add butter. Add eggs and cook. Mix eggs, sausage and cheese together.

Roll each biscuit into 4 ½ x 5 inch rectangle. Spoon 2 tablespoons of sausage mixture into each rectangle. Fold over and seal edges. Place on ungreased cookie sheet and bake in 400 degree oven for 12 to 15 minutes or until golden brown.

Chocolate Gravy

Ingredients:

½ cup cocoa

8 Tbsp. flour

½ cup plus milk

1 tsp vanilla

1 Tbsp. butter

½ cup sugar

Directions:

Combine dry ingredients in large skillet over medium heat, then add milk. Add more milk for desired consistency. Serve over biscuits with butter.

Hash Brown Breakfast Casserole

Ingredients:

1 pkg. frozen hash browns

1 doz. eggs, beaten

2 cups ham, diced small

½ cup onion, chopped

1 bell pepper, chopped

½ cup milk

1 ½ cups cheddar cheese, shredded

Salt and pepper to taste

Directions:

Sprinkle hash browns into well-greased 9" x 13" pan. Sprinkle ham, onions, bell pepper and cheese (in that order) over potatoes. Beat eggs, milk and seasonings well, then pour over. Bake at

350 degrees for 45 minutes to 1 hour...until set firm.

Corned Beef Hash

Ingredients:

½ stick butter

2 cups onion, small diced

1 Tbsp. garlic, chopped

1 ½ lb. corned beef, approx. 3 cups, chopped

1 ½ lbs. potatoes, peeled and small diced, approx.

3 cups

Directions:

Dice potatoes and add to boiling water to blanch.
Cook until soft on the outside, yet firm in the
middle. Remove from heat and put in cold water
for a few minutes.

Heat oil in an oven safe skillet over medium-high
heat and melt butter. Add the onions and season
with salt and pepper. Sauté until golden brown.
Add garlic and corned beef and continue to cook
for 2 minutes. Add the potatoes and continue to

cook for 4 minutes. Remove from heat and with spatula smash mixture into the pan. Place skillet in 400 degree oven for 8 to 10 minutes or until golden brown.

Bacon and Egg Muffins

Ingredients:

12 slices bacon

10 eggs

¼ cup milk

Salt and pepper to taste

½ cheddar cheese, shredded

Directions:

Cook bacon in microwave for 75 seconds. Place a slice of bacon into each cup of a muffin pan so the bacon goes around the cup.

Beat eggs and milk together and pour into cups. May top cups with chopped green onion, chopped red bell pepper or chopped jalapenos.

Bake at 375 degrees for 20 minutes. Top with cheese and bake for 5 more minutes or until cheese melts.

Taco Seasoning

Ingredients:

2 Tbsp. chili powder

1 Tbsp. cumin

2 tsp corn starch

2 tsp salt

1 ½ tsp smoked paprika

1 tsp coriander

½ tsp cayenne

Directions:

Mix all ingredients together and store in sealed container.

Egg Nog

Ingredients:

3 eggs, beaten

3 Tbsp. sugar

2 cups evaporated milk

2 cups water

Pinch of salt

1 tsp vanilla

Grated nutmeg

Directions:

Beat sugar into eggs, mix in evaporated milk, water, salt and vanilla. Served chilled or warm topped with whipped cream. Sprinkle with nutmeg.

Egg Nog

Ingredients:

6 large eggs, separated and at room temperature

1 pint of cold whipping cream

6 Tbsp. sugar

1 tsp vanilla

6 – 8 oz. bourbon

Nutmeg

Directions:

In large bowl, beat egg whites until they form soft peaks. In another bowl, beat whipped cream until it forms stiff peaks. Fold in egg whites. Place bowl in a larger bowl half filled with ice. Add egg yolks and beat. While beating, gradually add sugar and mix well. Add bourbon and continue beating. Gently fold in egg white mixture into the egg yolks and mix well. Chill. Sprinkle with nutmeg when serving.

Sweetened Condensed Milk

Ingredients:

1 cup powdered milk

1/3 cup boiling water

2/3 cup sugar

3 Tbsp.

Directions:

Combine all ingredients and mix well.

Play Dough

Ingredients:

2 ½ cups flour

½ cup salt

1 Tbsp. alum

2 cups boiling water

3 Tbsp. oil

Food coloring

Directions:

Mix all except food coloring. Separate into sections and color as desired.

Grandma's Salve

Ingredients:

1 lb. jar petroleum jelly

1 tsp turpentine
1 tsp eucalyptus oil
1 tsp carbolic acid
1 Tbsp. kerosene
1 Tbsp. white gasoline

Directions:

Mix all ingredients well. Use on burns and cuts.

Made in the USA
Columbia, SC
24 November 2022

72006126R00167